NATIONAL
GEOGRAPHIC
KiDS

DON'T READ THIS BOOK
Before Bed

Thrills, Chills, and HAUNTINGLY TRUE STORIES

ANNA CLAYBOURNE

NATIONAL GEOGRAPHIC
WASHINGTON, D.C.

CONTENTS

PAGE 24

PAGE 54

PAGE 126

PAGE 112

PAGE 98

THERE ARE LOTS OF THINGS WE UNDERSTAND ABOUT THE WORLD.

Most things in our world have sensible, scientific explanations, like where rain comes from, why tigers have stripes, and how airplanes fly. But then there are those other things—the unexpected, mysterious, **BAFFLING, AND CURIOUSLY CREEPY THINGS** that defy explanation! Weird events that no one understands. Mind-boggling questions that scientists still haven't been able to answer. And scary sights that people SWEAR they've seen, but that couldn't possibly be real ...

... or could they?

EASY EXPLANATION?

Lots of people are sure that even strange, paranormal, and spooky events have a simple, rational explanation. In some cases **A GHOST STORY OR SPOOKY SIGHTING COULD BE A HOAX, A RUMOR, OR A MADE-UP MYTH.** Or it could just be the result of someone's **OVERACTIVE IMAGINATION.** But ask the people who say these things have happened to them, and it's a different story! They're convinced they really **DID SEE A GHOST, MEET AN ALIEN, OR FOLLOW BIGFOOT** through the woods. So who's right? You'll have to read all about it, and judge for yourself!

IT'S ALL IN HERE!

So exactly what kinds of creepy curiosities might you encounter in the following pages? Well ...

- ⮞ Ghosts, vampires, and zombies; haunted houses; and creepy castles and cellars
- ⮞ Shudderingly scary real-life situations, chilling crypts, and other petrifying places
- ⮞ Weird, unexplained animal behavior that seems almost impossible
- ⮞ Crypto-creatures that may or may not exist, like Bigfoot, lake monsters, and the terrifying Mongolian death worm
- ⮞ Reports of alien spaceships flying by, and signs of life on other planets
- ⮞ People who say they can move things with their minds, or send messages directly into other people's brains
- ⮞ Strange, unexplained disappearances, and mysteries of science that will boggle your brain!

WHAT DOES "PARANORMAL" MEAN?

A lot of these odd and creepy topics are known as the paranormal. "Paranormal" means "alongside normal." It's the stuff that we all know isn't supposed to be real—but that a lot of people still believe. Although there are countless reports of people seeing ghosts, UFOs, mermaids, or the Loch Ness monster, it's often very hard to prove that things like this exist. That could be because they don't. Or it could be because they're very good at hiding!

Some scientists do try to study paranormal phenomena, and put them to the test. They sometimes come up with theories about why people believe in them, and what the scientific explanations could be. You'll find some of these theories in this book too.

Scared Silly

It's not much fun being scared out of your wits, is it? Actually, maybe it is! Why else would people go see spooky movies, sign up for ghost tours, or ... read this book? Scientists think it's because being really scared gives you an "adrenaline rush." Chemicals in your body make your heart pound and your muscles tense up. You breathe faster and feel ready for anything. This happens so that you can react and escape from real-life dangerous situations, like being chased by a crocodile. But if you're not really in danger—just listening to a creepy story or riding a roller coaster—you get to experience all this excitement in a safe way. Afterward, you feel full of relief and pride that you can handle the horror!

BLOOP BLOOP! WARNING!

It's not just a catchy title. If worrying about ghosts and ghouls, freaky phenomena, and haunted happenings keeps you up at night ... **DON'T READ THIS BOOK BEFORE BED!** Seriously, maybe you'd better put it down! Unless, of course, you like that kind of thing—which might be why you picked this book up to begin with. Okay ... proceed with caution. But if you don't know where you stand on the spooky spectrum, here something to keep in mind:

The topics inside are rated 1–10 on the handy fright-o-meter located on each spread. Look for this symbol to help you decide if you are ready to read at that level of scare before you continue reading. But what scares one person might not send one single chill down your spine. Or, maybe what someone else thinks is pretty tame sends you into a tizzy. So read on, but stop if that shadow in the corner starts to look an awful lot like the bogeyman.

ALL RIGHT, DON'T SAY WE HAVEN'T WARNED YOU. GO AHEAD, TURN THE PAGE ... IF YOU DARE!

HORRORS OF HOUSKA

FRIGHT-O-METER
DON'T READ THIS BOOK BEFORE BED
0 1 2 3 4 5 6 7 8 9 10
UWILLBUPALLN8

PLENTY OF CASTLES ARE SAID TO BE HAUNTED, BUT HOUSKA CASTLE MAY BE THE CREEPIEST OF ALL. To visit it, you'll have to go to the Czech Republic in Europe, travel deep into the countryside, and trek up a hill, through swamps and forests, far from roads, rivers, and towns. In fact, the mysterious castle is often said to be "in the middle of nowhere."

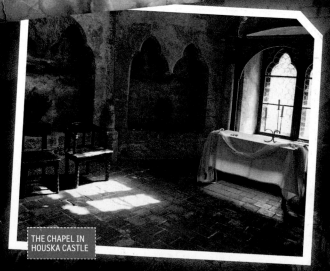
THE CHAPEL IN HOUSKA CASTLE

Entering the UNDERWORLD

Houska Castle was built more than 800 years ago, probably by local king Ottokar II of Bohemia, who placed it in a very strange and spooky spot. The castle was constructed over a huge, deep, dark hole in the ground. According to local legend, this hole was a gateway to the "Underworld." Many people believed it was bottomless—it was so deep that if you threw a stone into it, you would never hear it land. What's even creepier? Locals also claimed they had seen strange, black, leathery-winged creatures flying or crawling out of the pit.

No ESCAPE!

Houska Castle has all the makings of a horror movie. Middle of nowhere? Check. Creepy creatures? Check. A mysterious hole? Check. But perhaps the biggest mystery of all is that it doesn't seem to be designed for living in. It's not in a useful position for looking out for enemies, or guarding the surroundings. It was built in a place with no natural water supply, and it doesn't even have a kitchen. Even stranger, many of the windows you can see from the outside are fake. There are no rooms behind them, just solid stone. There are no stairs from the first floor to the upper levels. People had to climb to the second level using ropes.

Why would someone build such a useless structure? It's said the castle was built over the harrowing hole in order to block it, to protect the rest of the world from whatever might escape from it. Its walls weren't built to stop enemies from getting in, but to stop them from getting out!

MANY OF HOUSKA CASTLE'S WINDOWS ARE FAKE.

THE DANGLING Man

Today, the hole is still there, but you can't see it. It's completely covered over by the floor of the castle's chapel. But there's a spooky local legend about it dating from before the castle was built. According to the story, criminals who had been sentenced to death were offered a pardon if they agreed to be lowered down inside the hole, to see how deep it was and exactly what was inside it. One man agreed to the challenge, and was dangled down into the hole on a rope. But after just a few minutes, the people at the top heard him screaming in terror, and begging to be pulled back up. When he was hauled back to the surface, to everyone's horror, he looked completely different. He had become an old man, with snow-white hair, and a look of terror etched on his wrinkled face. He never recovered, and died soon afterward.

SPOOKY Sights

Like any good haunted castle, Houska is also said to be home to a number of hair-raising ghosts, which startled visitors have reported seeing. They include:

- ↪ **A huge, black, almost see-through monster** that's said to be a cross between a dog, a frog, and a human and to have a terrifying growl

- ↪ **A woman in a medieval-style dress** who wanders up and down the corridors, or peers out of windows (the ones that aren't fake!) in the top floor

- ↪ **A row of miserable-looking people, all chained together and guarded by big black dogs.** Several visitors claim to have seen a vision of them entering the castle gates

- ↪ **Screaming and wailing noises** coming from under the chapel floor, where the horrible hole still lies

GREAT HOLE OF FIRE

THOUGH HOUSKA'S GATEWAY TO THE UNDERWORLD HAS BEEN CLOSED OVER, THERE'S ANOTHER HOLE NICKNAMED THE "DOOR TO HELL" NOT TOO FAR AWAY. LOCATED IN TURKMENISTAN IN CENTRAL ASIA, THIS HOLE IS NOT ONLY IN THE MIDDLE OF THE DESERT, BUT IT'S ALSO FILLED WITH BURNING FLAMES. THE HOLE ITSELF IS 220 FEET (67 M) ACROSS AND ABOUT 100 FEET (30 M) DEEP, AND WAS MAN-MADE! IN THE 1970S, A HUGE CRATER OPENED UP WHEN SCIENTISTS WERE DRILLING, SEARCHING FOR NATURAL GAS RESOURCES. DANGEROUS GASES CAME SPEWING OUT OF IT, SO THEY SET IT AFLAME TO BURN THEM OFF. BUT THE GAS KEPT ON COMING, AND MORE THAN 40 YEARS LATER THE HOLE IS STILL ON FIRE. OOPS!

GREAT HOLE OF FIRE, DASHOGUZ PROVINCE, TURKMENISTAN

CREEPY CATACOMBS

IMAGINE WALKING WARILY DOWN A DARK, CHILLY, UNDERGROUND TUNNEL, WITH JUST A FLASHLIGHT TO GUIDE YOUR WAY. You can feel the walls close in around you. You get an uneasy feeling that eyes are looking at you. You point your light upward and you see it ... a skull staring back at you! You turn around to run, but you spot another! And another! HEEEEELLP!

It's not just a spooky story—this creepy place really does exist. Below the streets of Paris, the capital of France, there lies a huge network of underground passageways and rooms. They are known as the Catacombs of Paris, and they are home to a huge number of human bones—not hundreds or thousands, but *millions*.

DON'T READ THIS BOOK BEFORE BED
0 1 2 3 4 5 6 7 8 9 10
FRIGHT-O-METER
UWILLBUPALLNB

BONES ARE PRESERVED LONG AFTER FLESH ROTS AWAY, BECAUSE THEY ARE MOSTLY MADE OF STONE-LIKE MINERALS, SUCH AS CALCIUM.

CATACOMB CORRIDOR

NO BONES ABOUT IT

The passages were mostly created during medieval times, about 800 years ago. They were the by-product of stone excavation during the construction of Paris's great churches and palaces. Then, as Paris grew, streets and houses were built over the top, creating the tangled underground maze that remains today.

By the 1700s, Paris was a big, bustling city with hundreds of thousands of citizens. But in a time when life was hard and illness was rampant, the average life span was only around 40 years. The cemeteries were full to the point of bursting, and human bones began to stick up out of the ground or wash into people's gardens!

So city officials came up with a plan: move the bodies underground. They closed the cemeteries, and relocated millions of bones into the catacombs instead. The tunnels were blessed and made into holy ground, so that they could act as a burial site. Today, the catacombs contain the remains of around six million people—making it one of the biggest gravesites anywhere in the world.

DECORATING
THE DECEASED

When the bones were first moved, they weren't transplanted into individual graves—most were just thrown into the tunnels in a big pile. But in 1810 the city's leaders decided to make the catacombs a tourist attraction. They tidied up the tunnels and decorated them with carved stonework and signs. They also rearranged the bones themselves. Today, there are stacks of skeletal bits—skulls, forearms, femurs, and vertebrae—laid out in rows of symbols and patterns.

SKELETONS IN THE PARIS CATACOMBS

SPOOKY SLEEPOVER

Today, there are a few parts of Paris where you can see the catacombs firsthand. You can even take a guided tour! However, many of the tunnels are closed to the public—it's easy to get lost in the maze of creepy passageways. But that doesn't stop some locals, called cataphiles, from exploring the depths of the dead ends. These rebels illegally sneak into the catacombs through manholes or secret entrances. Some take lanterns and cooking gear, a supply of food, and their sleeping bags, and camp out in the skeleton-filled tunnels overnight! Those who don't fear the law have been known to hold a concert or a party in the catacombs' depths!

THE PRESERVED
MUMMIES OF PALERMO

IF YOU THINK SKELETONS ARE A BIT SPOOKY, WHAT ABOUT KEEPING ENTIRE DEAD BODIES ON DISPLAY UNDERGROUND, PRESERVED TO LOOK LIKE THEY DID WHEN THEY WERE ALIVE? IN PALERMO, ITALY, THERE ARE CATACOMBS FULL OF MUMMIFIED CORPSES, DRIED, EMBALMED WITH CHEMICALS, AND DRESSED IN THEIR BEST CLOTHES! THE PALERMO CATACOMBS LIE BENEATH A MONASTERY AND WERE ORIGINALLY THE BURIAL SITE OF MONKS. BUT WHEN WORD GOT OUT, LOCALS WANTED THEIR BODIES TO BE PRESERVED AND STORED THERE TOO. AND IT BECAME A FASHIONABLE CHOICE FOR THE DEARLY DEPARTED. EVENTUALLY, 8,000 BODIES ENDED UP IN THE CATACOMBS, AND YOU CAN STILL GO TO SEE THEM TODAY. (MAYBE YOU COULD EVEN BRING YOUR ... MUMMY!)

PALERMO CATACOMBS

THE MOTHMAN
AND THE OWLMAN

FRIGHT-O-METER

0 1 2 3 4 5 6 7 8 9 10

DON'T READ THIS BOOK BEFORE BED

UWILLBU ALLN8

THE STORY GOES: ON NOVEMBER 12, 1966, FIVE GRAVE-DIGGERS WERE AT WORK IN CLENDENIN, WEST VIRGINIA, U.S.A., WHEN THEY SAW SOMETHING VERY STRANGE. What looked like a tall, grayish brown man with huge wings took off from a nearby tree and swooped over them. Was it a human? Was it a bird? Was it an alien? No one knew—but it wasn't the last time people claimed to have seen the creepy creature.

MOTHMAN STRIKES AGAIN!

A short while later, in the nearby town of Point Pleasant, a group of friends were driving past an old explosives factory when they saw something spooky standing by the gate. It was taller than a man, with wings folded behind it, and glowing red eyes. Suddenly, it spread its huge wings, leapt straight up into the air, and flew after their car as they sped away.

In the next few months several people saw the flying monster, which was given the scary nickname "Mothman." All accounts of the creature are unsettling: It made electrical equipment malfunction, emitted a whining, shrieking noise, and even had pets running scared. One family claimed it peered into the windows of their house as they hid in terror!

TRADITIONAL NATIVE AMERICAN MYTHOLOGY TELLS OF A LEGENDARY GIANT MAGICAL BIRD CALLED THE THUNDERBIRD. PERHAPS PEOPLE IN POINT PLEASANT WERE AWARE OF THIS STORY, AND THIS MADE THEM THINK THEY WERE SEEING A HUGE MAN-BIRD CREATURE.

FORETELLING
MISFORTUNE

About a year after the original sightings, on December 15, 1967, tragedy struck in Point Pleasant, when a bridge collapsed over the Ohio River during rush hour. People and cars tumbled into the icy waters below. After that, reports of the Mothman stopped. It seemed to have disappeared. As a result, some people thought its visits must have been some kind of disaster warning or bad omen. And that was the end of that ... or was it?

THE OWLMAN OF MAWNAN

Almost a decade later, in 1976, something spookily similar happened—this time far away in Cornwall, England. Two young sisters, on vacation with their parents, were walking through the woods. It wasn't long before they saw something terrifying, hovering in the air above the tower of nearby Mawnan Church. One of the girls drew a sketch of what she had seen: a human-size gray creature with big wings, like a cross between a man and a bird.

EYEWITNESS DRAWING OF THE "MOTHMAN"

Three months after that, two teenagers who were camping in the same area spotted the bizarre beast again. At first they saw it standing on the ground, and they thought it was a person dressed in costume. Then, to their horror, it spread its wings and shot straight up into the sky, through the trees.

They too made sketches. They described the creature as man-size, with big wings, crablike claws, and glowing red eyes. It also made hissing, screening, or whining sounds. Awfully similar to the Mothman in West Virginia! But this time, the creature did not go away. It has popped up several times over the years, according to reports from locals and tourists. Whatever it was, or is, almost everyone who has claimed to have seen it has found it spine-tinglingly scary.

SO ... WHAT WAS IT?

SOME EXPERTS THINK AN EAGLE OWL COULD EXPLAIN THESE SPOOKY SIGHTINGS. EAGLE OWLS AREN'T AS BIG AS HUMANS—AT MOST, THEY GROW JUST OVER TWO FEET (0.6 M) LONG. BUT THEY DO HAVE LONG WINGS AND REDDISH EYES. IN THE DARK, OR FROM A DISTANCE, AN EAGLE OWL COULD LOOK BIGGER THAN IT REALLY IS.

OTHERS, THOUGH, THINK THESE STRANGE SIGHTINGS INDICATE SOMETHING GENUINELY PARANORMAL—SOME KIND OF CRYPTID CREATURE, OR EVEN AN ALIEN VISITOR. FOR NOW IT REMAINS A MYSTERY ... BUT KEEP YOUR EYES OPEN. YOU NEVER KNOW WHERE MOTHMAN WILL POP UP NEXT!

ROBERT THE DOLL

MOST KIDS HAVE HAD A DOLL AT SOME POINT IN THEIR LIFE, RIGHT? Maybe it was your favorite toy that you played with every day. Or maybe it was a family heirloom that sat in the corner of your room untouched. Well, what if one day you noticed that your doll's eyes seemed to follow you around the room? Or perhaps you swore you left it in one corner, but when you came back it was in another? Or maybe you just get a strange feeling that there's more to the doll than buttons and stuffing? Robert the Doll—to give him his full name—is a large, child-size doll that is more than 100 years old. Around the year 1900, he was given to a young boy named Robert Eugene Otto, known as Gene, in Key West, Florida, U.S.A. The doll became Gene's constant companion—the two were so inseparable, Gene named the doll after his real first name!

DON'T READ THIS BOOK BEFORE BED

0 1 2 3 4 5 6 7 8 9 10

FRIGHT-O-METER

UWILLBUPAL_NB

Creepy CONVERSATIONS

Gene's parents soon noticed that their son was strangely attached to Robert. He took him everywhere, and people overheard him holding long conversations with the doll. Robert would "reply" to Gene in a deep, scary voice—but it was just Gene pretending. *Wasn't* it!?

Sometimes Robert the Doll seemed to make a strange, spooky laughing sound. He would appear in a different place from where he had been put down. And people passing by the house swear they saw the doll come up to the window!

"Robert DID IT!"

One night, Gene's mother heard her son screaming in terror. She found him curled up under his blankets and trembling, with Robert the Doll sitting calmly on the foot of the bed, staring at him. The room was a mess, and the furniture had all been knocked over. Gene could only whisper, "Robert did it!"

Often, things in the house would be mysteriously destroyed or messed up, and Gene would say the same thing—"Robert did it!" Eventually, the family was so freaked out by the doll, they hid him in the attic ... only to be plagued by strange sounds and footsteps from above.

TOP: ROBERT EUGENE OTTO AND HIS WIFE, ANNE, IN 1961

BOTTOM: THE OTTO HOUSE

"Get Rid of **THAT THING!**"

Robert stayed in the attic for many years, and Gene grew up and left home, eventually becoming an artist. But when his parents died, they left him the house, and he moved back in. He rescued Robert, dusted him off, and began keeping the doll by his side again, just as he had done as a child. Gene's wife was not happy! She swore she could see the expression on the doll's face changing, and that it didn't like her. She persuaded Gene to put the doll back in the attic, but it would reappear in odd places around the house.

Finally, after Gene and his wife both died, another family moved into the house. They found Robert, and their 10-year-old daughter decided to keep him. Like Gene before her, she woke up screaming in the night and swore that she had seen the doll moving. She told her parents that Robert hated her and wanted to kill her. So her family got rid of Robert, donating him to a local museum.

JUST TO ADD TO THE CREEPINESS, ROBERT HAS LITTLE HOLES ALL OVER HIS FACE. THEY WERE PROBABLY MADE BY MOTHS WHEN HE WAS STORED IN THE ATTIC.

See for **YOURSELF**

Today, Robert the Doll is still at the Fort East Martello Museum in Key West, where he has his own glass box—and, according to visitors and staff, is still haunted. People say they have seen him move, and that his expression can change from an innocent smile to an angry scowl, or a pained look of sadness. People leave him bags of sweets, and some say he eats them! And even the staff are always polite to him ... just in case.

THE FORT EAST MARTELLO MUSEUM

ROBERT THE DOLL AS HE APPEARS TODAY

IF YOU WANT TO TAKE A PHOTO OF ROBERT AT THE MUSEUM, ACCORDING TO TRADITION, YOU NEED TO POLITELY ASK HIS PERMISSION. IF HE TILTS HIS HEAD SLIGHTLY, THAT MEANS YES!

WHO MADE **ROBERT?**

ACCORDING TO AN OLD LOCAL LEGEND, ROBERT THE DOLL WAS MADE BY A SERVANT GIRL WHO WORKED IN THE OTTOS' HOUSE, LOOKING AFTER GENE WHEN HE WAS A BOY. GENE'S PARENTS WERE SAID TO BE MEAN TO THEIR SERVANTS. SO THE GIRL MADE A DOLL FOR ROBERT, BUT PUT A CURSE ON IT TO GET HER REVENGE ON HER CRUEL EMPLOYERS. SOME SAY SHE SEWED TINY ANIMAL BONES INTO THE STUFFING INSIDE THE DOLL, OR THAT SHE CUT HAIR FROM GENE'S HEAD AND USED IT TO MAKE ROBERT'S HAIR.

ACTUALLY, THOUGH, THERE'S NOT MUCH EVIDENCE FOR THESE SPOOKY TALES. ANOTHER VERSION OF THE STORY SAYS THAT ROBERT WAS JUST A REGULAR DOLL MADE BY A TOY COMPANY, AND THAT HE WAS A GIFT TO GENE FROM HIS GRANDFATHER. TODAY, THERE'S NO EXACT RECORD OF WHERE HE CAME FROM.

PREDICTING A DISASTER

IN THE YEAR 1898, AMERICAN AUTHOR MORGAN ROBERTSON PUBLISHED A NOVEL CALLED *FUTILITY, OR THE WRECK OF THE TITAN.* In the story, a huge luxury passenger ship, the *Titan,* sets out across the Atlantic Ocean. But it sinks after hitting an iceberg, killing more than half of the passengers on board.

Sound familiar? That might be because something very similar actually happened in real life. The *Titanic,* a huge luxury passenger ship, sank after hitting an iceberg in the North Atlantic on her maiden voyage. More than 1,500 people died because there weren't enough lifeboats, and some that the ship did have were sent away less than half full.

You might be thinking ... so what? People write books based on true events all the time. But here's the spooky part: Morgan Robertson's book *Futility* was written 14 years before the real-life disaster in 1912, and several years before the *Titanic* was even built.

DON'T READ THIS BOOK BEFORE BED

0 1 2 3 4 5 6 7 8 9 10

FRIGHT-O-METER

UWILLBUPALLN8

THE R.M.S. *TITANIC* IN ITS FINAL RESTING SPOT

CRAZY COINCIDENCE?

Rationality tells us that Robertson didn't predict the future, and it was simply coincidence. But the author didn't just foretell the main details. There were all kinds of other creepy similarities in his book:

➲ Though Robertson was American, his ship the *Titan* was British—and so was the *Titanic*.

➲ The *Titan* was a steel ship with three propellers and two masts—like the *Titanic*. The *Titan* was 800 feet (244 m) long; *Titanic* was only a bit longer at 882 feet (269 m).

➲ In *Futility*, the *Titan* hits an iceberg in April, close to midnight, about 460 miles (740 km) from Newfoundland, on the starboard side of the ship. All these details matched the *Titanic* disaster exactly.

➲ In the book, there's a high death toll because the ship wasn't carrying enough lifeboats— exactly what happened in real life!

➲ The *Titan* is described as "unsinkable" in the novel—just as the real *Titanic* was (not very accurately in either case).

LIFEBOAT FULL OF SURVIVORS FROM THE R.M.S. *TITANIC*

HOW DID HE KNOW?

After the 1912 disaster happened, people thought Morgan Robertson must have psychic powers, and that he could somehow see into the future. But Robertson himself disagreed. He said he simply knew a lot about ships, and his predictions were based on the trends in shipbuilding at the time. So could all those details really have matched up just by chance? It seems amazingly unlikely—but so far, there's no other explanation.

FATAL FORECAST

Robertson wasn't the only person to anticipate the *Titanic* disaster. British newspaper editor William Thomas Stead wrote a similar short story in 1886. It was about a large steamship sinking in the Atlantic, with disastrous loss of life because there were not enough lifeboats. Stead claimed he was warning people about what could really happen, if the rules about lifeboats were not made safer. But it gets even stranger. William Thomas Stead didn't just predict the tragedy— he lived it. Stead was on board the *Titanic* when it sank! He died in the disaster at age 62, after helping other passengers into the lifeboats.

I'M NOT GOING!

DID SOME OF THE *TITANIC*'S OTHER PASSENGERS FORESEE THE DISASTER TOO? A LARGE NUMBER OF PEOPLE WHO WERE BOOKED ON THE VOYAGE—AT LEAST 60 OF THEM—CHANGED THEIR MINDS ABOUT GETTING ON BOARD. SOME REPORTED FEELING UNWELL, BUT OTHERS COULDN'T REALLY EXPLAIN THEIR HESITATION. SCOTTISH POLITICIAN NORMAN CRAIG WAS LOOKING FORWARD TO HIS TRIP, BUT CANCELED AT THE LAST MINUTE, SAYING, "I SUDDENLY DECIDED NOT TO SAIL, I CANNOT TELL YOU WHY ... AT PRACTICALLY THE LAST MOMENT, I DID NOT WANT TO GO." GEORGE AND EDITH VANDERBILT ALSO CANCELED, BECAUSE A FAMILY MEMBER WAS WORRIED ABOUT THEM GOING ON THE SHIP'S MAIDEN VOYAGE.

THE WRECK OF THE *TITANIC* WAS DISCOVERED ON THE NORTH ATLANTIC SEABED IN 1985, THE REMAINS OF THE SHIP LAY IN ICY COLD WATER 12,500 FEET (3,810 M) DEEP.

TERROR IN THE NIGHT

FRIGHT-O-METER
DON'T READ THIS BOOK BEFORE BED
0 1 2 3 4 5 6 7 8 9 10
UWILLBUFALLN8

YOU'RE LYING ON YOUR OWN BED, IN YOUR OWN BEDROOM. You know that you're awake—but you feel paralyzed—you can't move a muscle. You can't even open your eyes, however hard you try. Then, to your horror, you feel something starting to creep onto your bed, and right on top of you, until it's sitting right on your chest. You try to scream—but nothing comes out!

It sounds like the ultimate nightmare, right? Trapped with an eerie presence, unable to escape? But believe it or not, it's not uncommon—and while it's not real, it's not supernatural either. Instead, it's simply something that people's brains sometimes do, and it's called "sleep paralysis."

BRAIN BOGGLED

When you fall asleep, your brain switches off your consciousness, or awareness, so you don't notice what's happening around you. At the same time, it stops your muscles from moving too much, so that while you're asleep, you mostly stay still.

When you're just at the point of waking up or falling asleep, this system can malfunction. Your consciousness wakes up, but your muscles are still stuck, and you can't move. Your brain gets confused, and starts creating strange, spooky sensations.

The feeling that there's something climbing onto your bed or body is one of the most common effects. People from all around the world, and from many different times in history, have described the same thing. It's known as "old hag syndrome," because people used to believe the thing on your chest was a witch. Sometimes, though, it doesn't feel like a human figure, but like an animal or a goblin-like creature.

SOME PEOPLE CAN GET UP OPEN THEIR EYES, WALK AROUND, AND EVEN DO OTHER THINGS LIKE MAKING A SANDWICH—ALL WHILE THEY ARE ACTUALLY STILL FAST ASLEEP. IN THE MORNING, THEY REMEMBER NOTHING ABOUT IT.

FEELING SHAKY

Other people experience different effects from sleep paralysis. They can include a jangling, buzzing feeling in their chest, a sensation that the bed is shaking violently, or hearing scary voices. The good news is that none of it is real. After a few seconds or minutes, you wake up, you can move again, and the spooky visitors are gone. Phew!

SCARY SCIENCE

Some people have a different type of sleep problem that's just as creepy. Right in the middle of the night, they'll experience something called night terrors: Their body wakes up, but their mind keeps on having the dream—or nightmare—that they were having while they were asleep. When they open their eyes, they see the things they're dreaming about, right there in their bedroom! It could be a giant ice-cream cone or a fluffy cloud bed, but it could also be a pack of hungry wolves, a bottomless hole in the ground, or a scary creature that's chasing them. This is a type of hallucination—when your brain causes you to see something that's not really there. Not surprisingly, people this happens to can end up screaming or jumping right out of bed in a panic, waking up everyone else in the house.

SLEEPING AND DREAMING

IF YOU THINK ABOUT IT, GOING TO SLEEP EVERY NIGHT IS QUITE STRANGE. FOR AROUND 8 HOURS OUT OF EVERY 24—OR A THIRD OF YOUR ENTIRE LIFE—YOU FALL UNCON-SCIOUS AND HAVE NO IDEA WHAT'S GOING ON. SCIENTISTS THINK THE POINT OF SLEEP IS FOR YOUR BRAIN TO SORT THROUGH THE THINGS YOU'VE SEEN AND DONE, AND DECIDE WHAT TO REMEMBER AND WHAT TO FORGET. THIS HELPS YOUR BRAIN "ORGANIZE" YOUR MEMO-RIES, AND AVOID GETTING OVERLOADED. THAT'S WHY IF YOU STAY AWAKE FOR TOO LONG, YOU CAN GET REALLY CONFUSED. YOUR BRAIN CAN'T THINK CLEARLY, AND YOU START TO MAKE SIMPLE MISTAKES. IT'S ALSO THE REASON GETTING PLENTY OF SLEEP HELPS YOU LEARN BETTER. SLEEPING HELPS YOUR BRAIN STORE INFORMATION AND MAKES IT STICK IN YOUR MEMORY. AND IT EXPLAINS WHY DREAMS ARE OFTEN FULL OF ALL KINDS OF STUFF THAT HAPPENED TO YOU RECENTLY, ALL JUMBLED UP AND MIXED TOGETHER!

EXPLAIN THE UNEXPLAINABLE?

Sleep paralysis and night terrors are so com-mon that experts believe they could be the explanation behind ghost sightings, spooky events, and even stories of alien abduction. If people don't know that it's their half-asleep brain playing tricks on them, they could really believe that a ghost, witch, monster, or alien visited them in the night.

COULD UFO SIGHTINGS JUST BE DREAMS?

FLYING TRI

FRIGHT-O-METER
UWILLBUPALLN8

DON'T READ THIS BOOK BEFORE BED

0 1 2 3 4 5 6 7 8 9 10

UNIDENTIFIED FLYING OBJECT (UFO) SIGHTINGS ARE HARD FOR MANY PEOPLE TO BELIEVE. The night sky is so vast, how can people who spot a UFO be sure they didn't just see an airplane or a weather balloon? But when hundreds of people see the same thing, over a period of several months, it's a lot harder to explain. And that's what happened in eastern Belgium just a few decades ago.

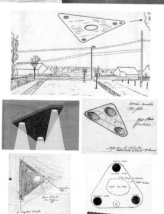

EYEWITNESSES MADE SKETCHES OF THE CRAFTS.

I SPY ...

THE SIGHTINGS BEGAN ON THE NIGHT OF NOVEMBER 29, 1989, WHEN TWO BELGIAN POLICE OFFICERS, Heinrich Nicoll and Hubert von Montigny, went to investigate a strange light. They were amazed to see a huge, flat, triangle-shaped object, with glowing lights at the corners, hovering above a field. They radioed a call for help back to the chief at their station, but not surprisingly, he didn't believe them. Until, that is, he saw something very similar sailing past his own office window.

Meanwhile, the object began to move, so the officers followed it in their patrol car. Soon, another similar triangle appeared and hovered next to the first, before zooming up into the sky and vanishing. A short time later, the first object flew away too.

A SERIES OF UFO SIGHTINGS OF THE SAME OR SIMILAR OBJECTS IS KNOWN AS A "WAVE." THE BELGIAN UFO WAVE IS PROBABLY THE MOST FAMOUS OF ALL.

A PHOTO SAID TO SHOW THE LIGHTS OF THE TRIANGULAR UFO

ANGLES

THE CHASE **IS ON!**

IT WOULD LATER SURFACE THAT SEVERAL OTHER POLICE OFFICERS, AND DOZENS OF OTHER PEOPLE, ALSO SAW BIZARRE, THREE-SIDED, SPACESHIP-STYLE UFOS THAT NIGHT. Over the next few months, they were spotted again and again. On March 30, 1990, there was another major UFO event. Two of the triangles were sighted, flying close together. This time they were detected on radar. The Belgians decided to send two F-16 fighter jets, capable of supersonic speeds, to chase them. But every time they got close, the triangles would zoom away—seemingly faster than any human-built aircraft could.

EYEWITNESS **ACCOUNTS**

People who saw the strange flying triangles often reported the same details.

- The UFOs had a light at each corner, and a light in the middle.
- The lights changed color at random.
- The triangles didn't fly like normal aircraft. They could hover in one place, move slowly, or rocket away at enormous speed.
- Depending on the report they were either silent, or only made a low, quiet humming sound.

ARTIST RENDERING OF A "FLYING TRIANGLE"

CLOSE **ENCOUNTERS?**

SOME SKEPTICS (PEOPLE WHO DON'T BELIEVE IN PARANORMAL EVENTS) SAY THE BELGIAN UFO SIGHTINGS CAN BE EXPLAINED AS A "MASS DELUSION." In other words, once people started talking about them, others also believed they could see them, but they were really just imagining it. However, the triangle-shaped craft were detected by radar systems too—so the fact is that there was something mysterious in the sky on those nights.

Others think that UFO sightings like this could also be explained as top secret military aircraft. Perhaps the government developed some kind of super-powered, silent flying machine, but kept it quiet so other countries would not catch on. However, the Belgian UFOs appeared decades ago, and there are still no known fighter aircraft that look like them. Experts believe it would be difficult to keep that kind of technology under wraps for so long.

To this day, the Belgian UFO "wave" is still one of the most widely witnessed, hardest-to-explain UFO events ever. Many people think it provides good evidence that nonhuman flying machines have visited our planet.

QUIZ

MoOOOOVING DAY!

BY NOW YOU KNOW THERE ARE DOZENS OF CREEPY CASTLES, haunted houses, and other bloodcurdling buildings in this book. So the burning question is: If you HAD to live in one of them, which would you choose? Follow our haunted house quiz to find the best hair-raising home for you!

DO YOU WANT A NICE BIG GARDEN WITH YOUR HAUNTED HOUSE?

NO | YES

DOESN'T MATTER

WOULD YOU LIKE A NICE VIEW TO LOOK AT WHILE BEING HORRIBLY HAUNTED?

YES

NO

ARE YOU GOOD AT CLIMBING WALLS? (OR MAYBE FLYING?)

YES | NO

WOULD YOU PREFER A SWIMMING POOL, OR DUNGEONS FOR DEALING WITH THOSE NUISANCE ENEMIES?

WOULD YOU RATHER BE HAUNTED BY GHOSTS, OR BLACK RUBBERY-WINGED DEMONS?

GHOSTS

DUNGEONS | POOL

DEMONS

HORRIFYING HOUSKA CASTLE

(SEE PAGE 8)
It's in the middle of nowhere, the windows are fake, there's no kitchen, and it's built over the gateway to the Underworld. Sounds like a ghastly getaway, but we hear the demons love it!

HAUNTED LEAP CASTLE

(SEE PAGE 125)
Who could resist this charming period property in the romantic Irish countryside? You're not bothered by ghosts galore, terrifying torture chambers, and a few stubborn bloodstains, are you?

SPOOKY STANLEY HOTEL

(SEE PAGE 36)
Good for those who are not gaga for ghouls—the ghosts at this classy country residence are very well-behaved. They'll even play the piano for you!

START HERE

DO YOU NEED CREATURE COMFORTS, LIKE A KITCHEN, RUNNING WATER, AND A COMFY BED?

WELCOME

NO ← → **YES**

DO YOU WANT TO LIVE NEAR STORES AND RESTAURANTS?

NO

YES

DO YOU MIND IF YOUR HOME HAS A DEADLY HISTORY?

NO

YES

DO YOU NEED A RESIDENCE FIT FOR A KING OR QUEEN?

YES → **TERRIBLE TOWER OF LONDON**
(SEE PAGE 74)
It's grand, historical, and has a fabulous London location to die for. But you'll need to be bold to brave this abode, as its spooks and specters can be seriously sinister.

NO

DO YOU LIKE MUSIC?

YES **NO**

DO YOU PREFER CLASSIC STONE CONSTRUCTION, OR SOMETHING MORE MODERN (SAY, BUILT IN THE LAST 250 YEARS)?

CLASSIC

MODERN

BONE-CHILLING BRAN CASTLE
(SEE PAGE 38)
Also known as Dracula's Castle, this ancient pile of rubble has tons of character and a spooky forest setting. Perfect as a holiday home, you might even want to spend eternity there ...

GHOST-PACKED WHITE HOUSE
(SEE PAGE 108)
Big, glam, and beautifully decorated, this is a fabulous luxury home that's great for entertaining world leaders. Hey, even the ghosts are famous!

THE MYSTERIOUS NASCA LINES

FRIGHT-O-METER
DON'T READ THIS BOOK BEFORE BED
0 1 2 3 4 5 6 7 8 9 10
UWIL..BUPALLN8

STRETCHING ACROSS A DUSTY DESERT IN SOUTHERN PERU, YOU'LL FIND A SPIDER AS BIG AS A SWIMMING POOL, A MONSTER-SIZE MONKEY, AND A KILLER WHALE THAT COULD SQUASH A WHOLE VILLAGE. Don't worry—they're not real—but they are incredible. These are the Nasca lines, made on the desert surface by ancient people who lived around 2,000 years ago. But who left them there? And why?

THE NASCA LINES ARE A UNESCO WORLD HERITAGE SITE. TO KEEP THEM SAFE, VISITORS ARE NOT ALLOWED TO WANDER THE DESERT WHERE THEY ARE FOUND BUT CAN TAKE A FLIGHT OVER THEM TO GET A GOOD VIEW.

AERIAL ENIGMA

WHY WOULD ANCIENT PEOPLE CARVE HUNDREDS OF THESE HUGE IMAGES AND MARKINGS SMACK-DAB IN THE MIDDLE OF THE DESERT? And better yet, how? To modern experts, there seems to be no connection between the images—from simple lines or geometric shapes, to plants, flowers, and animals. But what really leaves them scratching their heads is how people created neat, perfect shapes on such a grand scale. Standing on the ground, you can't really see the images properly; you need to view them from high above.

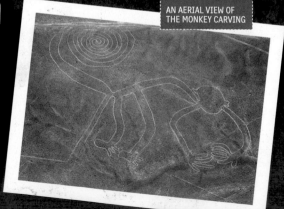

AN AERIAL VIEW OF THE MONKEY CARVING

HIGH IN THE SKY

LOCAL PEOPLE HAVE KNOWN ABOUT THE LINES FOR CENTURIES. But since outsiders discovered them in the 1920s, they've come up with some bizarre explanations for their existence. Perhaps the strangest idea is the theory that whoever created them did not do so from the ground. Is it possible, as some believe, that the lines were made by aliens as runways or landmarks to help them land their spaceships? Alternatively, some people say the Nasca people made the lines using ancient hot-air balloons or other aircraft, many hundreds of years before history tells us these things first appeared. Those who believe this theory think the Nasca must have invented flying machines long before modern times, but any evidence of them has been lost.

AN AERIAL VIEW OF THE HUMMINGBIRD CARVING

PECULIAR POSSIBILITIES

SKEPTICS POINT OUT THAT YOU CAN ACTUALLY SEE THE DESIGNS WELL ENOUGH FROM NEARBY HILLS. NO ONE HAD TO BE IN THE SKY TO MAKE THEM. INSTEAD, DOUBTERS HAVE COME UP WITH OTHER IDEAS ...

➲ **A guide to the stars and constellations.** Some of the lines match up with constellations in the night sky, so they could have been designed as a guide to the stars.

➲ **A calendar.** Some believe the pictures stood for different seasons, months, or other indicators of the passage of time.

➲ **Ritual pathways.** Perhaps the Nasca made the lines to walk along as part of their religious rituals. Many of them join up in a loop, so if you wanted to, you could walk around and around all day, without stopping or having to turn around.

➲ **We're here!** Or they could have been made to impress whatever gods the Nasca believed in, or just to mark the Nasca land as theirs.

THE CONSTELLATION ORION

MAKING THE NASCA LINES

WHEN YOU SEE THE NASCA LINES AND IMAGES FROM A DISTANCE, THEY LOOK LIKE LINE DRAWINGS MADE IN WHITE CHALK OR CRAYON ON A DARKER SURFACE. IN FACT, THE NASCA PEOPLE DIDN'T "DRAW" THE PICTURES AT ALL. THEY MADE THEM BY REMOVING A LAYER OF DARK PEBBLES FROM THE SURFACE OF THE DESERT, REVEALING THE PALER SAND UNDERNEATH.

IN MANY OTHER PLACES, THE LINES WOULDN'T HAVE LASTED LONG, AS RAIN AND WIND WOULD HAVE GRADUALLY FADED AND WASHED THEM AWAY. THE NASCA DESERT, THOUGH, IS VERY DRY, AND NOT VERY WINDY, SO THE LINES HAVE STAYED VISIBLE.

BUT HOW DID THEY MAKE SUCH BIG PICTURES SO NEAT, AND THE LINES SO STRAIGHT? THOUGH THEY LIVED A LONG TIME AGO, THE NASCA WOULD HAVE BEEN ABLE TO MEASURE DISTANCES, SO THEY COULD PLOT OUT THE MAIN POINTS OF A PICTURE ON THE GROUND BEFORE JOINING THEM TOGETHER, OR EVEN USE ROPE-LIKE MATERIAL TO CONNECT ONE POINT TO THE NEXT.

CACTUS CARVING

THE VANISHING LIGHTHOUSE KEEPERS

FRIGHT-O-METER
DON'T READ THIS BOOK BEFORE BED
0 1 2 3 4 5 6 7 8 9 10
UWILLBU4ALLN8

IT WAS MIDNIGHT IN THE DARK, FOGGY, FREEZING COLD NORTH ATLANTIC OCEAN, IN THE MIDDLE OF DECEMBER 1900. As the steamship *Archtor* sailed toward Scotland, it passed by the seven steep, craggy Flannan Isles, called the "Seven Hunters." Captain Holman was expecting the bright warning light that always shone from the lighthouse on the top of Eilean Mor, the tallest island. But on this night, it stood in darkness. Holman sailed quickly on to the Scottish mainland, where he reported that the light was not working. What happened to the three keepers who always manned the lighthouse on Eilean Mor?

THE LIGHTHOUSE ON EILEAN MOR

HESPERUS
TO THE RESCUE

Back then, there was no way to contact the men on the islands to find out if something was amiss—no email or phone, or even a telegraph cable. People on the much bigger Isle of Lewis, 20 miles (32 km) away, could use a telescope to try to see the islands, but they couldn't contact the men to find out why the light was out.

The only way to check on the lighthouse keepers was to sail out to the islands. The supply boat *Hesperus* was due to visit the Flannan Isles on December 20, taking food and letters, and another lighthouse keeper, Joseph Moore, to start his shift. But because of bad winter weather, it didn't actually make the trip until December 26.

Flannan Isles

SCOTLAND

LOCATOR MAP OF THE FLANNAN ISLES

DESERTED!

As the *Hesperus* drew close to Eilean Mor, everything was strangely silent. The flag was not flying. No men came out to greet the crew, the boxes for the supplies had not been left at the landing jetty, and when Captain James Harvey sounded the boat's horn, there was no response.

Replacement keeper Joseph Moore went ashore and hastily climbed the steep cliff pathway to the lighthouse, filled with an overwhelming sense of dread. There was no one to be seen anywhere on the tiny isle, and the lighthouse was empty. There was no fire in the grate. In the kitchen, everything was in order, except that one chair lay overturned. And Moore found only one set of oilskins (waterproof clothing) left behind. The other two sets were missing.

The keepers normally recorded the weather and their activities every day on a blackboard, then copied the notes into a log book. Moore found the records had been kept until 9 a.m. on December 15. That must be when all three men had vanished. But where had they gone?

LEFT TO RIGHT: THOMAS MARSHALL, DONALD McARTHUR, JAMES DUCAT, AND ROBERT MUIRHEAD

NO ONE HAS TO LIVE ON THE SPOOKY FLANNAN ISLES ANYMORE. THE LIGHTHOUSE BECAME AUTOMATIC IN 1971. PHEW!

FRIGHTFUL FATES

As reports of the men's disappearance spread, people came up with all kinds of eerie theories about what had happened to them:

➔ One keeper had gone mad and murdered the other two, before flinging himself into the sea.

➔ A giant seabird or even a sea monster had grabbed the keepers and dragged them away.

➔ The Phantom of the Seven Hunters, angry about a lighthouse being built on its home, had turned the three men into cormorants.

➔ A scary ghost boat had stopped there, and the ghosts had kidnapped the three men.

➔ More recently, some people have said aliens could have landed on the islands and abducted the unlucky keepers!

A MORE LIKELY STORY

SO WHAT REALLY HAPPENED? TO THIS DAY, NO ONE REALLY KNOWS—BUT THERE IS A LEADING THEORY THAT WOULD MAKE MORE SENSE THAN MADMEN AND ALIENS. INVESTIGATORS LATER FOUND ONE SIDE OF THE ISLAND WAS BADLY DAMAGED, AS IF A GIANT WAVE OR POWERFUL WINDS HAD BATTERED IT. THE ISLAND HAD A TRACK AND PULLEY SYSTEM FOR HAULING SUPPLIES UP THE CLIFFS, AND SOME OF ITS RAILS HAD BEEN RIPPED OUT OF THEIR CONCRETE BASE.

EXPERTS DECIDED A GIANT STORM HAD STRUCK THE ISLAND. TWO OF THE MEN HAD GONE OUT IN THEIR OILSKINS TO SECURE EQUIPMENT, TO STOP IT FROM BEING DAMAGED. THE RULES STATED THE LIGHTHOUSE COULD NOT BE LEFT UNATTENDED, SO ONE STAYED BEHIND. BUT HE MUST HAVE SEEN SOMETHING THROUGH THE WINDOW—PERHAPS A HUGE WAVE APPROACHING—AND RUN OUT, WITHOUT HIS OILSKINS, TO WARN THE OTHERS. IF HE WAS TOO LATE, ALL THREE MEN WOULD HAVE BEEN WASHED INTO THE SEA.

BURIED ALIVE

FRIGHT-O-METER
DON'T READ THIS BOOK BEFORE BED
0 1 2 3 4 5 6 7 8 9 10
UWILLBUPAL~N8

IMAGINE WAKING UP ONE MORNING IN TOTAL DARKNESS. There's no light; you can't see a thing. You breathe deeply and the air you exhale immediately hits your face. There's something right above you. A wall? Well, yes, of sorts. Realization rushes over you. You scream for help but realize no one is going to hear you. There's nothing you can do. You are buried six feet (1.8 m) underground. Your stomach twists into knots as you await your fate and wonder how long you have left ... Being buried alive sounds like the plot of a scary movie, but believe it or not, it wasn't too long ago that this nightmare scenario could happen in real life!

Wake THE DEAD

Doctors can usually tell when a person has died—but not always. They check for signs of life, like breathing and a pulse. But sometimes, these are so faint that they can't be detected, especially if the person is in a coma—a deep, unconscious state caused by illness or injury. In some cases, people can wake up from a coma, and recover. If they've been buried in the meantime, they're in big trouble!

This was even more of a problem long ago, when we didn't have as many doctors, not to mention the modern hospitals and medical technology we have now. Hundreds of years ago, people often died without seeing a doctor at all, and were buried by their families or friends. And mistakes really DID happen ...

A GRAVESITE THAT HAS BEEN OPENED

DEAD RINGER

IN THE 1700S, DOCTORS AND SCIENTISTS BEGAN WRITING ABOUT CASES LIKE THESE. THEY BECAME MORE COMMON DURING OUTBREAKS OF DISEASES LIKE CHOLERA AND YELLOW FEVER, WHICH CAUSE VICTIMS TO FALL INTO COMAS. IN THE 1800S, HORROR WRITER EDGAR ALLAN POE BEGAN TO INCLUDE TALES OF LIVE BURIALS IN HIS SPOOKY GHOST STORIES.

OVER TIME, PEOPLE BECAME MORE AND MORE CONCERNED THAT IT MIGHT HAPPEN TO THEM. THE SOLUTION? INVENTORS CAME UP WITH VARIOUS DESIGNS FOR "SAFETY COFFINS." THESE SPECIAL COFFINS HAD DEVICES THAT A (NOT) DEAD PERSON COULD USE TO ALERT THE OUTSIDE WORLD TO THE FACT THAT THEY WERE, IN FACT, STILL ALIVE.

THIS COFFIN, DESIGNED BY DR. JOHANN TABERGER, HAD ROPES ATTACHED TO THE BODY'S HANDS AND FEET, LEADING TO A BELL ABOVE THE GROUND. IF YOUR BODY WRIGGLED, THE BELL WOULD RING!

IF THE **FEAR** OF BEING BURIED ALIVE **SCARES YOU** TO DEATH, YOU'RE **NOT** ALONE—IT'S CALLED TAPHOPHOBIA.

Six Feet UNDER

Stories of people who weren't actually dead when they were buried date back for centuries.

- ➲ **Thomas à Kempis** 15th-century Dutch monk and writer Thomas à Kempis was buried in 1471, after appearing to be dead. He was later dug up, and, according to legend, there were scratch marks on the inside of the coffin, and splinters under his fingernails.

- ➲ **Madam Blunden** Buried in England in 1672, Madam Blunden was thought to be dead as a doornail. But young boys playing near her grave said they heard screams! At first no one believed them, and the poor lady was not rescued in time. When she was finally dug up, she was dead, but evidence revealed that she had tried to escape her coffin prison.

- ➲ **Mr. Jenkins** In North Carolina, U.S.A., in 1885, a man with the last name Jenkins "died" of a fever, and was buried, even though some people thought he looked quite healthy! Some time later, they dug up the body, just to check. The body had turned over, its hair had been pulled out, and the lid of the coffin had been pushed open and was covered in scratches.

- ➲ **Josef Guzy** It has happened in more recent times too. In 2010, a beekeeper from Poland, Josef Guzy, was lying in his coffin, awaiting his burial. Then, the undertakers noticed he seemed to have a pulse! He was rescued and, even though he had had a heart attack, eventually made a full recovery.

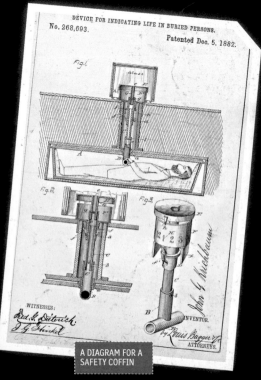

A DIAGRAM FOR A SAFETY COFFIN

LURKING IN THE LAKE

FRIGHT-O-METER
DON'T READ THIS BOOK BEFORE BED
0 1 2 3 4 5 6 7 8 9 10
UWILLBUI ALLN8

IN A.D. 565, AN IRISH MONK NAMED COLUMBA WAS VISITING SCOTLAND WHEN HE WITNESSED A STRANGE SIGHT. At the River Ness, he came upon a group of people burying one of their friends, who they said had been attacked by a water beast. Columba asked a man named Lugne to swim across the Ness to test whether their story was true. As he did so, a huge water monster emerged and grabbed Lugne in its jaws. Columba, who must have commanded great authority, ordered the monster to stop and to return to the depths, which it did.

At least, that's how the story goes! This ancient tale about

COLUMBA

Columba is said to be the first ever sighting of the Loch Ness monster, or "Nessie"—a creepy cryptid rumored to live in Loch Ness, a large lake in Scotland. In the years since Columba ordered the monster to the depths of the lake, it's been "spotted" many times but has never bitten anyone again.

NERVOUS NESSIE

THIS FAMOUS PHOTOGRAPH, TAKEN IN 1934, CONVINCED MANY PEOPLE THAT NESSIE WAS REAL. BUT THE PHOTOGRAPHER, SHORTLY BEFORE HIS DEATH, ADMITTED IT WAS A FAKE.

SINCE THE FIRST SIGHTING THERE HAVE BEEN MORE THAN A THOUSAND EYEWITNESS REPORTS OF THE LOCH NESS MONSTER. Nessie is often described as having a long neck and tail, but a very small head. She has a humplike back that can sometimes be seen sticking up out of the water. Some people have described seeing several humps in a row. That could mean the monster has a series of humps—or that they actually saw a family of Nessies swimming along together!

Since the invention of the camera, "Nessie seekers" have tried to capture the beast on film. There are quite a few famous photos of the neck and head sticking up from the water, but most have been proven to be hoaxes. Others could be explained by natural debris, such as a log or sticks. One person theorized that people are actually seeing a Wels catfish—which can grow up to 400 pounds (181 kg)!

Still, enthusiasts remain unconvinced. Loch Ness is so deep that it could easily hide dozens of lake monsters! And, it's true, since satellites have been used to scan Earth and make maps, some strange shapes have shown up in Loch Ness. Maybe something is out there after all ... at least we know it doesn't bite!

CHAMP

"CHAMP" IS THE NICKNAME OF THE MONSTER OF LAKE CHAMPLAIN, WHICH LIES IN THE STATES OF NEW YORK AND VERMONT, U.S.A. Like other lake monsters, Champ has been spotted many times by enthusiastic tourists or cryptid hunters. In both 1873 and 1945, boaters enjoying a day on the lake reported spotting the monster swimming along the surface.

An even more famous sighting occurred in the summer of 1977, when Sandra Mansi stopped at the lake with her family. Her children were playing in the water when she suddenly saw the head and neck of a huge animal emerging from the lake. She managed to take a picture, which is now known as one of the most convincing lake monster photos of all.

"CHAMP" THE LAKE MONSTER OF LAKE CHAMPLAIN

PREHISTORIC PHENOMENA?

A LOT OF THE WORLD'S LAKE MONSTERS LOOK VERY SIMILAR—AND VERY FAMILIAR! THEY TEND TO RESEMBLE PLESIOSAURS, ANCIENT WATER REPTILES THAT LIVED IN THE TIME OF THE DINOSAURS. THEIR FEATURES OFTEN INCLUDE A PLESIOSAUR-LIKE LONG NECK, SMALL HEAD, AND HUMPED BACK, AND SOMETIMES FLIPPERS. IN FACT, SCIENTISTS HAVE WONDERED IF SMALL GROUPS OF PLESIOSAURS COULD HAVE SOMEHOW SURVIVED EXTINCTION IN DEEP LAKES, AND CONTINUED EXISTING TO THIS DAY. IF THEY HAVE, IT WOULD BE AN AMAZING SCIENTIFIC DISCOVERY. BUT THE MONSTERS SEEM TO BE SO GOOD AT HIDING, NO ONE HAS YET BEEN ABLE TO CATCH ONE.

OGOPOGO FEATURED ON A POSTAGE STAMP

CANADA 39
THE OGOPOGO L'OGOPOGO

OGOPOGO

ANOTHER FAMOUS LAKE MONSTER MIGHT LURK UP NORTH. Ogopogo is said to inhabit Okanagan Lake in western Canada. In 1926, it made a public appearance when it was spotted by dozens of tourists, who all agreed they had seen it. Several people have filmed strange ripples and large, long shapes moving through the water. Ogopogo is usually described as a long, sea serpent–like creature with a bumpy body and a head like a goat or a horse.

MYSTERY LIGHTS

IN A VALLEY NEAR PAULDING, MICHIGAN, U.S.A., YOU CAN SEE A STRANGE LIGHT GLOWING AT NIGHT. It flickers, sways, and bobs up and down in midair, looking just like a lamp carried by an invisible person. According to local folklore, it's the ghost of a railway engineer who was hit by a train and still haunts the area, carrying his lantern.

But is the truth even stranger than fiction? Ghostly lights are not an uncommon occurrence in North America.

In Texas, the mysterious Marfa lights hover and dart to and fro on the horizon. On the border between Oklahoma and Missouri, you can look out for the scary, color-changing Spooklight, said to be a poor ghost of a man who lost his head and still goes searching for it! And near St. Louis in Saskatchewan, Canada, a light roams up and down an old, abandoned railway track—giving it the spine-chilling nickname the "St. Louis Ghost Train."

DON'T READ THIS BOOK BEFORE BED

0 1 2 3 4 5 6 7 8 9 10

FRIGHT-O-METER

UWILLBUPALLN8

A VALLEY IN NORWAY, CALLED HESSDALEN, HAS ITS OWN **SPOOKY LIGHTS.** THEY SEEM TO BE CAUSED BY ELECTRICITY, LIKE EARTHQUAKE LIGHTS.

HESSDALEN LIGHTS

WEIRD SCIENCE

It all sounds very spooky indeed. Are these lights really ghostly lanterns, trains, or other supernatural specters? After all, many people claim that ghosts show up on photographs as glowing orbs or balls of bright light.

Well, you might be relieved to hear that investigations *have* found an explanation for "ghost" lights like these—or some of them, at least. Investigators have found that the Paulding light, the Spooklight, and some sightings of the Marfa lights could be caused by cars moving along distant highways in the dark.

As the cars come up a hill, they beam their headlights up into the air. The light bends back down toward the ground, or "refracts," as it shines through different layers of air in the atmosphere. This means the light can be seen somewhere else, even when the cars themselves are out of sight. It's the same effect that causes a mirage in the desert. People testing this theory have checked to see that the lights appeared at the same time the cars drove by. They did!

IN SCANDINAVIAN FOLKLORE, A WILL-O'-THE-WISP WAS SAID TO SHOW WHERE YOU COULD FIND FAIRY TREASURE.

GHOSTLY ORBS

WILL-O'-THE-WHAT?

Science can also explain other eerie lights witnessed throughout history. Long ago, people believed that if you saw an eerie, bluish, flickering light in a damp forest or a marsh, it was a magical lantern carried by a fairy or mischievous goblin. If you tried to get closer to it, it seemed to move away. This meant the goblin was trying to lead you astray to make you get lost.

This kind of light is known as a will-o'-the-wisp, and it has been seen all over the world. Today, though, we know that the lights are not that magical after all. They are caused by natural gases emitted by damp, rotting plants. When they rise into the air, they can burst into flames and glow for a short period of time.

EARTHQUAKE LIGHTS

FLASHING, RIPPLING, COLORFUL BRIGHT LIGHTS SOMETIMES APPEAR ON THE GROUND OR IN THE AIR JUST BEFORE AN EARTHQUAKE (OR SOMETIMES, A VOLCANIC ERUPTION). FOR A LONG TIME, SCIENTISTS DIDN'T THINK THEY REALLY EXISTED, ALTHOUGH PEOPLE REPORTED SEEING THESE EARTHQUAKE LIGHTS OR "EQLS." BUT THEY HAVE NOW BEEN CAUGHT ON FILM, AND THEY ARE MOST CERTAINLY REAL! EXPERTS THINK EQLS ARE CREATED WHEN ROCKS PUSHING AND SCRAPING TOGETHER CREATE A STRONG ELECTRICAL CHARGE. IT'S A LITTLE LIKE LIGHTNING, BUT MADE IN THE GROUND, INSTEAD OF IN THE CLOUDS.

33

THE DEVIL'S FOOTPRINTS

FRIGHT-O-METER
DON'T READ THIS BOOK BEFORE BED
UWILLBUPALLN8

IN DEVON, ENGLAND, THE NIGHT OF FEBRUARY 7, 1855, WAS CLOUDY, DARK, AND VERY COLD. When people woke up the next morning, they were not surprised to find the landscape covered in snow. They were, however, surprised to find something else: the Devil's footprints, or at least, that's what they came to be called. They were spooky-looking tracks that someone—or something—had left in the snow overnight while most people slept. A curious animal or a person wandering through the wilderness? Perhaps. However, they stretched over a distance of a hundred miles (161 km)—a lot farther than most people or animals could walk in just a few hours. And the spook factor doesn't end there ...

A PERPLEXING PATH

The footprints were deep and U-shaped, like a horseshoe. But they were much smaller—only about two inches (5 cm) across—and very close together. They formed a long, thin line, one foot stepping right in front of the other, with only about eight inches (20 cm) from one step to the next. They looked very much like a track left by a two-footed creature—but at the same time, they were definitely not human footprints.

Spooky enough to make you rethink going outside alone at night? Well, here's the part that will really have you hiding under the covers: The tracks of the mysterious footprints followed a path that defied the laws of physics. No ordinary creature could possibly have left such a trail.

- ➜ They led up to a haystack, disappeared—and then continued on the other side.

- ➜ They led to a drainpipe on the side of a house—then straight over the roof, and started again on the far side.

- ➜ They seemed to pass right through solid walls, leaving the snow on top of the wall untouched!

- ➜ They crossed people's gardens and went up to their front doors, even when the gardens were surrounded by high walls, and their gates were locked.

- ➜ The tracks led straight to the River Exe, which was very wide, and started again on the other side.

SPOOKY FOOTPRINTS IN THE SNOW. BUT WHO MADE THEM?

A MAGICAL MYSTERY?

As the creature that made the tracks seemed to have some kind of magical powers, many people started to think that a supernatural presence had visited Devon that night. They thought the footprints looked as if they could have been made by the cloven (split) hoofs of some sort of devilish creature.

But after the story of the frightening footprints was reported in the newspapers, many people came forward with other theories.

"IT WAS A KANGAROO!"
It turned out two kangaroos had recently escaped from a zoo nearby. Unfortunately, the footprints were nothing like kangaroo tracks. Not even from a small kangaroo.

"IT WAS A BALLOON!"
Another idea was that a hot-air balloon had passed by, dangling a rope which made the marks. But if that were the case, it's very unlikely that they would have been so neat and regularly spaced.

"IT WAS A BADGER!"
British scientist Richard Owen, who was famous for his dinosaur fossil discoveries, decided the tracks were made by a badger. The ice had then thawed and refrozen, partly melting the prints to give them their strange shape. But how could a badger possibly travel that far?

"IT WAS JUST A HOPPING RAT."
One reader wrote to a London newspaper to say the tracks were obviously made by a rat hopping along with its feet together.

As many explanations as people dreamed up, none of them really made much sense. And so, to this day, the curious case of the Devil's footprints remains a mystery.

SOMETHING SMELLS FISHY

IN 1953 AND 1954, TWO PECULIAR ANIMALS WERE WASHED UP ON THE BEACH ON CANVEY ISLAND IN ESSEX, ENGLAND. WHEN SCIENTISTS INVESTIGATED THEM, THEY COULDN'T FIGURE OUT WHAT THEY WERE. THEY WERE SAID TO HAVE PINKISH BROWN SKIN LIKE A HUMAN'S; TWO BIG, STICKING-OUT EYES; SHARP TEETH; GILLS LIKE A FISH; AND, WEIRDEST OF ALL, TWO LEGS. THE LEGS HAD NARROW FEET, EACH WITH FIVE TOES ARRANGED IN A U-SHAPE. COULD THIS HAVE BEEN THE CREATURE THAT MADE THE FREAKY FOOTPRINTS?

DEVIL'S TRAMPING GROUND!

In North Carolina, U.S.A., there's a mysterious place known as the Devil's Tramping Ground. It's a circle of land in the woods where no plants will grow—not even grass.

According to local legend, that's because another evil creature walks around in a circle there at night. They say if you leave a stone in the circle, it will have been kicked out of the way by morning!

HAUNTED HOTEL

FRIGHT-O-METER
DON'T READ THIS BOOK BEFORE BED
0 1 2 3 4 5 6 7 8 9 10
UWILL IUPALLN8

WELCOME TO THE STANLEY HOTEL IN ESTES PARK, COLORADO, U.S.A., WHERE YOU CAN ENJOY FRESH MOUNTAIN AIR, SKIING, HIKING, FINE FOODS ... AND GHOSTS IN YOUR BEDROOM! Spook seekers will love this vacation destination: This humongous hotel is one of the world's most famous haunted houses.

THE GLAMOROUS GHOST

THE STANLEY HOTEL WAS CONSTRUCTED BY ITS NAMESAKE, FREELAN OSCAR STANLEY, IN THE EARLY 1900s. He was a wealthy inventor who, along with his twin brother, Francis, invented the Stanley Steamer, an early motorcar. When Stanley was in his fifties, he moved to the Rocky Mountains in the hope that the fresh air would cure his tuberculosis (TB), a dangerous lung disease. However, he missed his lavish lifestyle back on the East Coast. There was only one thing to be done: Stanley decided Estes Park must be the site for a fabulous hotel decked out with every modern convenience of the time—running water, electricity, and gas lighting.

The Stanley Hotel opened its doors in 1909, and it wasn't long before it became a mountain hot spot. In fact, the town was practically built around it. In 1940, when Freelan Stanley died, it seems he couldn't bear to leave his mountain paradise. So he stuck around. Staff say they have spotted his ghost in the hotel's offices and lobby. They think that perhaps he likes to check that everything is running smoothly, and welcome new guests! He is rumored to also hang out in the bar area and billiard room, which were his favorite places when he was alive.

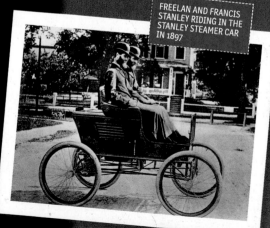

FREELAN AND FRANCIS STANLEY RIDING IN THE STANLEY STEAMER CAR IN 1897

STANLEY STAIRCASE

MUSICAL MYSTERY

FREELAN STANLEY'S NOT THE ONLY ONE HAUNTING HIS HOTEL—HIS WIFE, FLORA, IS SAID TO APPEAR ON THE MAIN STAIRCASE ALONGSIDE HER HUSBAND, BOTH DRESSED UP FOR A PARTY! Flora was a talented pianist. In addition to helping run the hotel, she would play music for the guests. People have heard her ghostly playing coming from the piano in the ballroom, even when no one is there. When anyone goes into the room, the music stops.

FRIGHT IN 407

ROOM 407 IS SAID TO BE HAUNTED BY YET ANOTHER GHOST, THAT OF THE EARL OF DUNRAVEN. He owned the land the hotel stands on before Freelan Stanley bought it from him around the year 1907. Eyewitnesses have reported seeing him standing in the corner of the room, the smell of his pipe filling the air. Even spookier, some people say they have seen his bad-tempered face staring out of the window of room 407 when no one is there.

FUN ON THE FOURTH FLOOR

IF YOU STAY ON THE HOTEL'S FOURTH FLOOR, YOU MIGHT NOT GET A VERY GOOD NIGHT'S SLEEP. If the thought of ghosts doesn't keep you awake, sounds of them might! Guests often claim to hear children shouting, giggling, and running up and down the corridors, all night long—even when there are no children staying in the hotel at all! Additionally, in room 418, staff say they have seen the shapes of invisible people lying on the beds.

Despite its dozens of ghost sightings, most of the staff at the Stanley don't seem to be frightened away. They say the ghosts are friendly and mean no harm!

TERROR IN 217

ONE OF THE MOST HAUNTED PLACES IN THE HOTEL IS REPORTEDLY ROOM 217. In 1911, it was the site of a huge explosion. The lamps had gone out, and a chambermaid named Elizabeth Wilson was sent to relight them. Unbeknownst to her, there was a gas leak, and—BOOM! The room (and several others nearby) blew up, sending debris, furniture, and the poor chambermaid crashing down into the dining room below. Luckily, she survived with just two broken ankles. But, after her death years later, she is said to have returned to haunt the room.

People who dare to book room 217 report lights switching themselves on and off, and doors opening and closing. Some guests say their blankets have been pulled off their beds in the night. Guests who go out often return to find their suitcases unpacked, and their clothes neatly folded. Haunting and helpful!

THE REAL-LIFE DRACULA

HE SLEEPS IN A COFFIN, CAN TURN HIMSELF INTO A BAT, AND SINKS HIS FANGS INTO HIS VICTIMS' NECKS TO SUCK THEIR BLOOD. Today, Count Dracula is a classic figure in movies, books, and even cartoons. After all, vampires are the stuff of legends, right? Maybe, but it turns out there was once a real Dracula, and in this case, it seems the man is even creepier than the myth.

Beyond THE BOOK

The Count Dracula we know now first appeared in 1897, in a horror novel by writer Bram Stoker. In the story, Dracula is an undead vampire, several hundred years old. He leaves his castle in Transylvania to invade Britain, and attacks, captures, and terrifies people, but is finally defeated.

Stoker based his book on folklore from Eastern Europe, which told of dead bodies that would rise from their graves and bite living people, sucking their blood or even eating them. However, the character of Count Dracula himself was inspired by someone else—a real-life, gruesomely violent king known as Vlad the Impaler.

PHOTO FROM THE 2014 MOVIE *DRACULA UNTOLD*

BACKGROUND: BRAN CASTLE

THE POENARI FORTRESS, ONCE OWNED BY VLAD DRACULA. DON'T WORRY, THE VICTIMS SHOWN HERE ARE DUMMIES.

VLAD,
Good or Bad?

Vlad the Impaler was one of the most vicious, violent rulers the world has ever known. He's said to have had up to 100,000 people murdered in the most revolting way possible—by impaling them, or sticking spikes right through them, and leaving the evidence for all to see. Even the toughest of Vlad's enemies were horrified by the gruesome spectacle of rotting, impaled bodies. However, in Vlad's homeland, he's often remembered as a hero—a brave leader who fought hard to protect his people.

Vlad lived in the 1400s, about 600 years ago. He wasn't actually from Transylvania, which is part of modern-day Romania. He was King Vlad III of nearby Wallachia. At that time, tiny Wallachia was surrounded by big, powerful kingdoms that could easily crush it. To keep them at bay, Vlad III would impale any prisoners of war he caught, and stick them on display on their spikes to warn other leaders not to mess with him. He also impaled wealthy landowners and merchants who tried to control the royal family—and anyone in Wallachia who broke his extremely strict laws. He was known to deliver his cruel brand of justice in other ways too, such as cutting off people's noses or other body parts.

Vlad's violent tactics worked—he managed to rule his kingdom, on and off, for many years. But while those who remained on the right side of him might have revered him as a good guy, he REALLY wasn't very nice. According to stories about him, he actually enjoyed torturing and killing people. It's said he would sit and eat his dinner surrounded by impaled corpses. And when one of his enemies imprisoned him for a while, he impaled the rats that he found in prison, as there were no other victims available.

VLAD THE IMPALER

DRACULA'S
CASTLE

IN PRESENT-DAY ROMANIA, YOU CAN VISIT BRAN CASTLE (SEE PHOTO ABOVE), WHICH IS ALSO KNOWN AS DRACULA'S CASTLE. IN FACT, THIS CASTLE DOESN'T HAVE MUCH TO DO WITH THE REAL VLAD DRACULA, ALTHOUGH HE MAY HAVE VISITED IT. IT DOESN'T HAVE MUCH TO DO WITH BRAM STOKER'S BOOK, EITHER. IT DOESN'T EVEN SEEM TO BE ESPECIALLY HAUNTED! BUT IT IS QUITE CREEPY-LOOKING, PERCHED ON A MISTY HILLSIDE, SURROUNDED BY FORESTS. THANKS TO ITS REPUTATION, THOUSANDS OF TOURISTS VISIT IT EVERY YEAR.

THE REAL VLAD DRACULA DID OWN SEVERAL OTHER CASTLES, THOUGH. ONE OF HIS FAVORITES WAS A CLIFF-TOP FORTRESS CALLED POENARI CASTLE. TODAY, IT MOSTLY LIES IN RUINS, BUT YOU CAN STILL VISIT IT—IF YOU DON'T MIND CLIMBING 1,480 STEPS TO GET THERE!

THE Dragon Family

But where did the name Dracula come from? Vlad III's father, Vlad II, was a member of a secret order (or group) of knights, the Order of the Dragon. He was given the name Vlad Dracul, meaning Vlad the Dragon. So his son, Vlad III, was called Vlad Dracula, meaning Vlad the Dragon's son. Bram Stoker thought this name sounded suitably spooky, so he borrowed it for his bloodthirsty vampire.

JELLY FROM SPACE

IMAGINE GOING FOR AN EARLY MORNING WALK AND STUMBLING ACROSS MYSTERIOUS WHITE GOO HEAPED ONTO THE GRASS LIKE SOME SORT OF GIANT GHOST BOOGER. Well, keep your eyes peeled after a meteor shower and you just might. For centuries, people have been finding revolting, gloopy, jellylike stuff appearing on the ground, as if from nowhere—especially first thing in the morning. They found the weird goop most often after seeing shooting stars, so they named it "star jelly" ... and to this day it continues to baffle scientists.

FRIGHT-O-METER
DON'T READ THIS BOOK BEFORE BED
0 1 2 3 4 5 6 7 8 9 10
UWILL8UPALLN8

SUNNY WITH A CHANCE OF GOO

ONE WRITER FROM THE 1600s, HENRY MORE, WROTE, "THOSE FALLING STARRES, AS SOME CALL THEM, WHICH ARE FOUND ON THE EARTH IN THE FORM OF A TREMBLING JELLY, ARE THEIR EXCREMENT." In other words, More thought the strange jelly was actually star poop! Other people think there's a more reasonable explanation. You know, something to do with aliens. But whether it's star poop or alien snot, the weird blobs of jelly still keep appearing around the world all the time. They range from pea-size up to soccer ball–size, sometimes even bigger. They are usually whitish or clear, but can be yellow, green, or even a purplish color.

Most star jelly pops up in small amounts here and there. But in Oakville, Washington, U.S.A., in 1994, it actually rained star jelly! The small, whitish, wobbly blobs fell all over the town, splatting down onto people's cars, homes, and gardens. One night in 1996, a meteor lit up the sky near the town of Kempton in Australia. The next day, people found sticky, slimy star jelly on the streets and sidewalks. In 2009, people in several parts of Scotland found lumps of star jelly in the grass. And in 2011, it was spread over hillsides in the Lake District, a part of England. So the real question is—what in the world (or out of this world) is it?

STAR JELLY HAS MANY OTHER WEIRD NICKNAMES TOO:
ASTRAL JELLY, STAR ROT, STAR SHOT, AND MOON POOP!

THE BLOB FROM OUTER SPACE?

SINCE THE JELLY APPEARS ON THE GROUND AFTER METEOR SIGHTINGS, PEOPLE DECIDED IT MUST HAVE DROPPED FROM THE SKY. However, stars are not made of jelly. They are made of gas and burning plasma. Furthermore, stars do not poop—and if they did, their poop wouldn't fall to Earth, as stars have their own powerful gravity.

Shooting stars, or meteors, however, do fall toward Earth. They are bits of rock or dust that get sucked in by Earth's gravity, then burn up and glow as they zoom through Earth's atmosphere. As this happens, though, they get very hot. Any jellylike substance on them would immediately vaporize. So it's extremely unlikely that star jelly really does come from space objects, or even falls from the sky at all.

BLARGH! WHAT IS THAT?

MITCHELL'S REED FROG EGGS

GOO GUESSES

THERE ISN'T JUST ONE SCIENTIFIC THEORY FOR STAR JELLY—THERE ARE SEVERAL! AND EACH ONE IS WEIRDER THAN THE NEXT:

FROG GUTS: Rather revoltingly, some star jelly seems to be from dead frogs. When female frogs lay their frog spawn, the eggs are covered in jelly. The frogs make this jelly inside their bodies. If a frog gets caught and eaten by a predator, such as a heron, the whitish jelly could spill out. If it gets wet, it swells up and grows.

NOSTOC: This is a type of bacteria that forms green, jellylike lumps when it gets damp. It's most likely to appear on your lawn after it's been raining. It looks gross, but it's actually harmless and has been used as food in the past.

WATER CRYSTALS: Water crystals or beads are a recent invention. They are tiny beads that can soak up lots of water and swell to many times their size—and when this happens, they look like a clear jelly. They are used to make disposable diapers, and to hold water in plant pots. If they get onto the ground and get rained on, they'll look like star jelly.

SLIME MOLDS: Slime molds are single-celled creatures similar to bacteria. Sometimes, many of them can stick together and form a kind of wobbly, slimy mass. They are often found in grass, so that could explain some "star jelly" discoveries.

SLIME MOLDS ARE ACTUALLY PRETTY CREEPY! A MASS OF MOLD DOESN'T HAVE A BRAIN, BUT IT CAN SNIFF OUT FOOD AND SLITHER TOWARD IT.

THE MUMMY'S CURSE

FRIGHT-O-METER

DON'T READ THIS BOOK BEFORE BED

0 1 2 3 4 5 6 7 8 9 10

UWILLBUALLNG

WHEN ARCHAEOLOGIST HOWARD CARTER OPENED TUTANKHAMUN'S TOMB IN 1923, IT CAUSED A MEDIA FRENZY. It was one of the few ancient Egyptian tombs to be found still filled with treasures, as well as the young pharaoh's coffin, his stunning golden death mask, and his mummified body. The tomb's permanent resident came to be known as King Tut, and some people believe the misfortune that befell those who entered his chambers is no mere coincidence.

STOP THE PRESSES!

In April 1923, just weeks after Tut's tomb was opened, the newspapers ran a sensational headline. Lord Carnarvon, the wealthy aristocrat who had paid for Carter to carry out the excavation, had suffered a sudden death. He had succumbed to a deadly infection after being bitten on the cheek by a mosquito, then cutting the swollen bite with his razor while shaving. Immediately, people began saying that Carnarvon was the victim of a terrible ancient curse, placed by the ancient Egyptians on anyone who disturbed their royal graves.

HOWARD CARTER (LEFT) AT THE ENTRANCE TO THE TOMB

KING TUT'S MUMMY

A RE-CREATION OF
TUT'S BURIAL
CHAMBER

TOMB OF DOOM

Carnarvon was just the first of many victims of the supposed mummy's curse:

- Wealthy American George Jay Gould died of a fever following a visit to Tut's tomb.

- Ali Kamel Fahmy Bey, an Egyptian prince, was murdered in London after visiting the tomb.

- Howard Carter's secretary, Richard Bethell, was found dead in his bed—possibly murdered.

- Richard Bethell's father, Lord Westbury, then died falling from the window of his London apartment, where treasures from the tomb were said to be kept.

- Next to go was Lord Carnarvon's half-brother, Aubrey Herbert. He died after a dental operation went horribly wrong.

- King Tut's mummy was sent to be x-rayed. The man who did the x-raying, Sir Archibald Douglas Reid, died shortly thereafter of a mystery illness.

- And the curse didn't only affect humans! According to some reports, Howard Carter's pet canary died on the very day the tomb was opened. Some say it was eaten by a cobra—an ancient emblem of the pharaohs!

- Another story claimed that when Lord Carnarvon died in Egypt, his pet dog, back home in England, died at the same moment.

Some said Howard Carter had found an eerie inscription in the tomb, warning that a curse would strike down anyone who entered it. Reluctant to abandon his adventure, he had hidden the message so as not to scare anyone. However, no evidence has been found for this, and it may be just a rumor.

CURSE, OR CHANCE?

The idea of a curse protecting pharaohs' tombs wasn't a new idea. Even back then, it was well-known in Egypt. So does that mean a curse really does befall those who dare to enter? People who have investigated King Tut's curious curse don't think it's quite as spooky as it seems.

There were literally thousands involved with Tut's tomb in one way or another—diggers and cleaners, museum workers, journalists, photographers, visitors, and tourists. Taking everyone into account, it's not so strange that a few of them would die over the next few years.

Plus, in the 1920s, people didn't have access to the medicine we do today. Doctors now believe Lord Carnarvon died of erysipelas—a bacterial infection that is easily treatable today. In 1923, many modern medications had yet to be discovered, and it was quite common to die of infections and fevers.

And what about Howard Carter himself? He was the one who actually started searching for the tomb, discovered it, and had it opened up. Surely he should have been first on the angry mummy's list. Yet Carter actually lived for another 13 years.

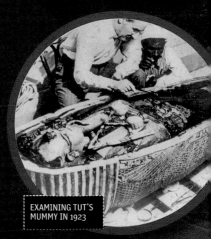

EXAMINING TUT'S
MUMMY IN 1923

KING OR PHARAOH?

TUTANKHAMUN IS OFTEN KNOWN AS KING TUT, BUT HE WAS REALLY A PHARAOH, NOT A KING. ANCIENT EGYPTIAN PHARAOHS WEREN'T JUST RULERS—THEY WERE ALSO REGARDED AS HALF HUMAN AND HALF GOD.

TELEPATHIC TWINS

TELEPATHY IS THE ABILITY TO SEND MESSAGES TO ANOTHER PERSON USING YOUR MIND—OR TO PICK UP SIGNALS ABOUT WHAT IS HAPPENING TO SOMEONE FROM AFAR. When scientists try to test for telepathy in a lab, they usually find no evidence of it. Yet there are a few incredible cases in which twins seem to be able to share information with each other—sometimes without even realizing it.

FRIGHT-O-METER
UWILLBUPALLN8
DON'T READ THIS BOOK BEFORE BED

HOW COMMON ARE TWINS? ON AVERAGE, IT'S ABOUT 30 OUT OF EVERY 1,000 PEOPLE.

SEPARATED AT BIRTH

Sometimes, twins are born and then adopted by two different families. They grow up apart from each other, often not even knowing that the other twin exists. In several cases, separated twins have been reunited later in life ... and found that their lives have been spookily similar! The most incredible case of all is the story of the "Jim twins" from Piqua, Ohio, U.S.A.

The Jim twins were born in 1940. When they were four weeks old, they were adopted by two families living about 40 miles (64 km) apart. Both families decided to name their new son "Jim," so one twin became Jim Lewis, and the other became Jim Springer.

Each boy knew he was a twin, but one of them, Jim Springer, grew up thinking his twin had died. When they were 37, Jim Lewis decided to search for his brother, looking through legal records to find out his twin's name. They finally met up in 1979, 39 years after they last saw each other. And that's when they discovered how many eerie similarities they had:

➲ Both Jims had owned a pet dog, which they both gave the unusual name Toy.

MIND MESSAGES

Many other twins, especially identical ones, tell stories of how they just "knew" something was happening to their twin, even if they were far away. Parents of twins often report this too.

A woman named Paula Wombwell, who has two identical twins, Katherine and Heather, tells the story of her twins' telepathy. She is a teacher and was in the classroom one day with Heather, while the other, Katherine, was in the school gym. Suddenly, they heard crying, and Heather explained that Katherine had been run over with a scooter—she even told her mom who did it! She was right—yet there is no way she could have possibly seen it happen.

In 2003, Richard and Damien Powles volunteered to participate in an informal experiment on twin telepathy that showed a seemingly undeniable physical connection between the two. Richard was put in one room with a bucket of freezing ice water, Damien was put in another and hooked up to a polygraph machine—which detects changes in heart rate. With no notice or warning, Richard would plunge his hand into the ice water, giving his body a mild shock. At another point, he was instructed to open a large box that contained a toy snake that jumped out at him. Both times, at the exact moment, noticeable "blips" occurred on Damien's polygraph readout—as if he had just experienced the same shocks. Could these things really just be incredible coincidences?

THE POWER OF TWO

THOUGH SOME PEOPLE BELIEVE IN TELEPATHY, IT'S VERY DIFFICULT TO PROVE. EVEN TWINS WHO SAY THEY HAVE A TELEPATHIC "LINK" FIND IT HARD TO SEND EACH OTHER MIND MESSAGES OR SIGNALS DURING LAB EXPERIMENTS. INSTEAD, IT SEEMS TO HAPPEN WHEN THERE'S A FEELING OF PAIN OR PANIC, WHICH THE OTHER TWIN CAN SOMEHOW SENSE. OR, AS IN THE CASE OF THE JIM TWINS, IT'S AS IF THEY COULD SOMEHOW SHARE PREFERENCES, SUCH AS NAMES AND HOBBIES, WITHOUT EVEN KNOWING IT.

TWINS OFTEN HAVE A VERY CLOSE SIBLING CONNECTION. THEY SPEND A LOT OF TIME TOGETHER, INCLUDING BEFORE THEY ARE BORN, SO IT'S NOT SURPRISING IF THEY UNDERSTAND EACH OTHER DEEPLY OR FEEL STRONG EMPATHY. BUT THAT DOESN'T EXPLAIN HOW THEY COULD KNOW SOMETHING ABOUT THE OTHER TWIN THAT THEY COULDN'T POSSIBLY HAVE FOUND OUT ANY OTHER WAY.

THERE ARE MILLIONS OF TWINS IN THE WORLD, SO MAYBE THINGS LIKE THIS JUST HAPPEN BY CHANCE, ONCE IN A WHILE.

THE WEST AFRICAN COUNTRY OF BENIN HAS THE HIGHEST TWIN BIRTH RATE IN THE WORLD—TWICE AS MANY AS MOST COUNTRIES.

- Both Jims had married wives named Linda. Both marriages had ended—and then both twins married women named Betty!

- Jim Lewis had a son named James Alan. Jim Lewis had a son named James Allan.

- They both loved math at school, but were bad at spelling.

- Both Jims had had jobs as sheriffs.

- Both Jims loved woodworking, and both had set up a wood workshop in their garages.

- They preferred the same make of car—a Chevy.

- They both drove their Chevys to the same part of Florida for family holidays.

- Both Jims had a terrible nail-biting habit and suffered from headaches.

Despite these incredible coincidences, there were some differences. Though they looked very similar, they had different hairstyles, and one had married a third time, whereas the other hadn't.

JIM LEWIS (LEFT) WITH JIM SPRINGER (RIGHT), UNDERGOING TESTS THAT SCIENTISTS HOPED WOULD FURTHER UNDERSTANDING OF ENVIRONMENTAL EFFECTS ON DEVELOPMENT

ANCIENT ASTRONAUTS

HAVE YOU EVER SEEN AN ALIEN? OR WITNESSED A UFO TOUCHING DOWN? IT MIGHT SOUND LIKE SCIENCE FICTION, AND MAYBE IT IS. But each year thousands of people claim they've seen, met, or been abducted by aliens, or even that they've gone for a ride on their spacecraft. You might think it odd that these reports only became common in the 1950s, when humans first began to explore space. In fact, the phrase "flying saucer," used to mean a UFO or alien spacecraft, was first invented in 1947—less than 100 years ago. But some people claim there's proof of alien existence that dates back further—hundreds, even thousands of years ago. But you won't find it in a science lab ... to check out these alien oddities, you'll need to visit an art museum.

DON'T READ THIS BOOK BEFORE BED

0 1 2 3 4 5 6 7 8 9 10

FRIGHT-O-METER

UWILLBUPALLN8

A BIRD MODEL FOUND IN AN EGYPTIAN TOMB IS SAID TO HAVE WINGS AND A TAIL LIKE A MODERN AIRPLANE. SOME SAY THIS MEANS THE EGYPTIANS INVENTED AIRCRAFT THOUSANDS OF YEARS AGO!

CASE STUDY #1:

ROCK ART ASTRONAUTS

In Brescia, in northern Italy, there's a huge collection of pictures and symbols carved into the rocks—more than 200,000 of them! They were made over a long time period, from about 10,000 years ago up until about 2,000 years ago. Some of the images look spookily similar to modern astronauts. The figures in this carving, for example, seem to be wearing "space helmets," and are even holding what could be some kind of high-tech astronaut gear. Others are said to look like aliens.

BRESCIA ROCK CARVING

NASCA LINE ASTRONAUT

ANCIENT EGYPTIAN AIRCRAFT

BESIDES ALIEN ASTRONAUT VISITORS, PEOPLE LONG AGO SEEM TO HAVE HAD ALL KINDS OF USEFUL AIRPLANES AND OTHER FLYING MACHINES—AT LEAST IF YOU BELIEVE SOME STORIES. THIS RELIEF CARVING, FOUND IN A TEMPLE DATING FROM MORE THAN 3,000 YEARS AGO, SHOWS SOME STRANGE OBJECTS THAT REALLY DO LOOK LIKE A HELICOPTER, AN AIRPLANE, AND SOME KIND OF AIRSHIP OR TANK.

EGYPTOLOGISTS SAY THIS IS ACTUALLY JUST A RANDOM SET OF MARKS, CAUSED BY THE EGYPTIANS CARVING VARIOUS DIFFERENT HIEROGLYPHS, OR SYMBOLS, ON TOP OF EACH OTHER.

CASE STUDY #2: ASTRONAUT OR FISHERMAN?

The Nasca lines are a set of huge, ancient markings on the ground in Peru (see pages 24–25). Some people have suggested they could have been created as runways or signs to help aliens land their spaceships. Experts don't really agree with this idea—but believers are still convinced by one image known as the "astronaut"—or sometimes, the "Nasca Owlman." The "astronaut" is about 100 feet (30 m) tall, and marked onto the side of a hill. His big, wide head and buglike eyes, not to mention his arm pointing to the sky, do make him look like an astronaut. However, skeptics say that he's actually holding a fish and a fishing net, and is a fisherman.

NATIVE AMERICAN PICTOGRAPH, UTAH, U.S.A.

CASE STUDY #3: ALIEN GIANTS

Sego Canyon, in Utah, U.S.A., has a huge range of rock art dating back thousands of years. It was created by generations of Native Americans who lived here in ancient times. Besides some human figures, there are all kinds of much bigger (and creepier) creatures. Some have huge eyes, or no eyes at all. Some have antennae, long tentacles, or weird wings. UFO fans say this is proof that something not of this world stopped off in Utah to say "Hi!" Could the pictures really show visitors from space? Or, as others claim, could they just be monsters that someone imagined or dreamed about? Take a look and see what you think!

"THE MADONNA WITH SAINT GIOVANNINO," 15TH CENTURY

CASE STUDY #4: MADONNA AND SPACESHIP

In this painting, which dates back to the 15th century, a man in the background is looking at a bizarre object in the sky. According to art historians, it's an angel that looks like a glowing cloud. But "ufologists" beg to differ, saying it's a spaceship. If it is, it's an angel that looks spookily like modern depictions of UFOs!

FISH PEOPLE

IN THE YEAR 1842, THE CITY OF NEW YORK WENT MERMAID-CRAZY. Rumors swirled around that a mysterious explorer, Dr. Griffin, had arrived in town, and had with him the preserved body of a real mermaid, caught near the islands of Fiji in the South Pacific. The newspapers went wild, and the famous showman P. T. Barnum did all he could to persuade Dr. Griffin to display the strange specimen to the public. At last, Griffin agreed, and thousands of people paid to view a real mermaid for the first time in history.

So was this proof that mythical mermaids really do exist!? Sadly, no, it wasn't. The whole thing was a clever hoax. The "Fiji mermaid" had come from eastern Asia, where Japanese fishermen often made mermaid models by stitching a monkey's head and upper body to the back end of a fish. Sailors had bought and sold it, until it fell into the hands of P. T. Barnum himself. "Dr. Griffin" was actually Barnum's accomplice, Levi Lyman. They used their fake story to whip up interest in the Fiji mermaid, then made a fortune charging the public to see it.

Still, when you look at the "mermaid," you can't help being gripped by curiosity and excitement at the idea that something so strange could really be swimming around in the sea. Could mermaids really exist?

THE "FIJI MERMAID"

SIREN SONG

Tales of mermaids date back to ancient times. The Mesopotamian civilization worshipped a god, Dagon, who was half human and half fish. Ancient Greek myths and legends tell of mermaid-like sea creatures called Nereids. There were also the deadly sirens, mythological female creatures who lived on a rocky island strewn with dead bodies. They sang a song so beautiful and irresistible that sailors would be drawn to the island and be unable to leave. Eventually, they would starve to death.

Over the centuries, sailors have reported seeing real mermaids in the waves, or on rocky shores. Perhaps due to the ancient tales of sirens, mermaids were thought to be a bad omen. The famously frightening pirate Blackbeard—a man so menacing he wore burning candles in his beard to scare his enemies—was terrified of mermaids. He believed they brought bad luck, and he instructed his crew to avoid "enchanted waters" where mermaids might be lurking.

One of the most notable mermaid-spotters was none other than famous 15th-century explorer Christopher Columbus. During one of his trips from Europe to the Caribbean Sea, he believed he and his crew saw mermaids. Columbus wrote in his log that he saw three "sirens" near the island of Hispaniola, but that they were not as beautiful as they appeared in books, although they did have humanlike faces.

MERMAID SCULPTURE, ROMAN ARC DE TRIOMPHE, CA 20 B.C.

A PAINTING OF TWO MERMAIDS

MERMAIDS ARE THOUGHT TO HAVE A FISHLIKE TAIL, BUT IN 1943, JAPANESE SOLDIERS REPORTED SEEING HUMANLIKE SEA CREATURES WITH TWO LEGS AND PINK SKIN.

FACT OR FISHY?

SO, COULD THERE REALLY BE MERMAIDS OUT THERE? IT'S UNLIKELY—WOULDN'T ONE ACCIDENTALLY GET CAUGHT IN A FISHING NET FROM TIME TO TIME, OR HAULED ABOARD A BOAT IN A CASE OF MISTAKEN IDENTITY? WOULDN'T WE FIND THEIR BODIES OR SKELETONS WASHED ASHORE, AS CAN HAPPEN WITH FISH AND WHALES? BECAUSE THERE IS NO SOLID EVIDENCE LIKE THIS, MOST SEA-LIFE EXPERTS BELIEVE MERMAIDS ARE JUST A MYTH.

MEANWHILE, FRIGHTENING PHOTOS OF "REAL" MER-PEOPLE CONTINUE TO SURFACE FROM VARIOUS SOURCES ON THE INTERNET, BUT THESE SCARY-LOOKING SNAPS AND VIDEOS ARE USUALLY QUICKLY PROVEN TO BE FAKE. IN FACT, THERE WAS AN ENTIRE DOCUMENTARY DEVOTED TO MERMAIDS THAT CAME OUT IN 2011, WHICH TURNED OUT TO BE A HOAX.

LOOKS REAL, BUT IT'S A HOAX

WAS THAT A MERMAID?

IT'S THOUGHT THE MERMAIDS CHRISTOPHER COLUMBUS SPOTTED COULD ACTUALLY HAVE BEEN DUGONGS—GRAYISH, FRIENDLY-FACED SEA MAMMALS SIMILAR TO MANATEES.

QUIZ

ARE YOU A GOOD GHOSTBUSTER?

IN THIS BOOK, YOU'LL MEET ALL KINDS OF SPOOKY SPECTERS and supernatural beings. But if you were to meet them in real life, would you have a clue what to do? Test your skill with this ghoulish ghostbusting quiz, and find how good you'd be at defeating the dark forces of the para-normal. Good luck—you're going to need it!

BEWARE: *Of course, a lot of people don't believe in ghosts, ghouls, vampires, or zombies at all. Maybe you don't either. And these methods of dealing with them have definitely NOT been scientifically tested. But just in case anything spooky should happen to exist, we've gathered the best advice from folklore, urban myths, old wives' tales, and scary movies!*

1 WHAT'S THE BEST WAY TO GET RID OF A GHOST?

A. Get a pet cat.
B. Spray your entire house with perfume.
C. Make a trail of candy leading out of the door.
D. Politely ask it to leave.

2 WHICH SMELLY FOOD IS SAID TO SCARE VAMPIRES AWAY FROM YOUR HOME?

A. A warm tuna melt sandwich
B. A hard-boiled egg
C. A bulb of fresh garlic
D. A slice of stinky cheese

3 WHAT COLOR SHOULD YOU NOT WEAR IN ORDER TO AVOID ATTRACTING THE MYSTERIOUS MONGOLIAN DEATH WORM?

A. Pink
B. Yellow
C. Black
D. Purple with orange spots

4 HOW CAN YOU AVOID BEING CHASED BY A WEREWOLF?

A. Don't go out at night when there's a full moon.
B. Eat plenty of chocolate.
C. Carry a daisy with you at all times.
D. All of the above

5 WHAT'S THE BEST WAY TO KEEP FAIRIES HAPPY, SO THAT THEY DON'T WRECK YOUR HOUSE?

A. Leave out a bowl of milk or cream for them.
B. Give them a dollhouse to live in.
C. Grow mushrooms in your garden.
D. Hang a teaspoon on your front door.

7 WHILE AT SEA, HOW CAN YOU AVOID BEING LURED TO YOUR DEATH BY THE IRRESISTIBLE SONG OF THE SIRENS?

A. Cover your ears with slices of bread.
B. Sing an even louder song yourself.
C. Have yourself tied to the mast of your boat.
D. Wear a bird around your neck.

6 HOW DO YOU KEEP WITCHES AWAY AT NIGHT?

A. Play loud rock music.
B. Sprinkle coffee grounds around your house.
C. Hang up a stone with a hole through it.
D. Draw a star on your doorstep.

ANSWERS:

1. WHAT'S THE BEST WAY TO GET RID OF A GHOST?
D. Politely ask it to leave. It's simple! Ghosts often seem to be quite reasonable, and it's said they will go away if you just ask them nicely.

2. WHICH SMELLY FOOD IS SAID TO SCARE VAMPIRES AWAY FROM YOUR HOME?
C. A bulb of fresh garlic. Vampires just hate garlic! Make sure you have plenty of it around, and they'll run away, holding their noses.

3. WHICH COLOR SHOULD YOU NOT WEAR IN ORDER TO AVOID ATTRACTING THE MYSTERIOUS MONGOLIAN DEATH WORM?
B. Yellow. This is said to be the Mongolian death worm's favorite color, so if you wear it, you may find the poison-squirting, electricity-zapping worm coming toward you.

4. HOW CAN YOU AVOID BEING CHASED BY A WEREWOLF?
A. Don't go out at night when there's a full moon. Werewolves only appear when there's a full moon, so this one is easily solved. Just stay in!

5. WHAT'S THE BEST WAY TO KEEP FAIRIES HAPPY, SO THAT THEY DON'T WRECK YOUR HOUSE?
A. Leave out a bowl of milk or cream for them. Fairies love to play tricks and make a mess, but if you give them some milk, they'll let you off the hook.

6. HOW DO YOU KEEP WITCHES AWAY AT NIGHT?
C. Hang up a stone with a hole through it. A stone with a hole in it is sometimes called a hagstone, or witch stone. It's said to have magic powers that scare witches away.

7. WHILE AT SEA, HOW CAN YOU AVOID BEING LURED TO YOUR DEATH BY THE IRRESISTIBLE SONG OF THE SIRENS?
C. Have yourself tied to the mast of your boat. This was the method used by ancient Greek hero Ulysses, according to Homer's famous Odyssey. It worked!

HOW MANY DID YOU GET RIGHT?

 0–2: YOU'RE GHOST TOAST

Unfortunately, you're not much of a match for supernatural forces.
Run and hide!

 **3–5: NOT BAD FOR A BEGINNER**

Your ghostbusting skills should save you, but there's room for improvement.

6–7: GHOSTBUSTER GENERAL!

When you're around, ghosts and monsters should be afraid—very afraid!

THE GLOWING FIREBALL

IT WAS A COLD, DAMP SUNDAY IN OCTOBER 1638, AND A HUGE THUNDER-STORM WAS RAGING OVER WIDECOMBE IN DEVON, ENGLAND. Inside the village church, local people huddled in fear as the storm rumbled and the sky grew darker and darker. Then, suddenly, the church filled with blinding light as a huge ball of fire burst in through the window, and floated through the building!

The glowing fireball, said to be eight feet (2.4 m) across, moved among the terrified crowd. It set light to people's clothes, burned their skin, and threw several of them to the ground. Then, as quickly as it had appeared, the fireball was gone, leaving the church filled with smoke and a strong smell of sulfur. Those lucky enough to survive were left with horrible burns and injuries.

FURIOUS FORCE

It sounds like a tall tale, something supernatural or imaginary. But scientists think this is actually an early report of a weird but natural phenomenon called ball lightning. Ball lightning is similar to regular lightning in that it is caused by electricity, but it behaves very differently. It's very rare, but when it does happen, it's normally during a thunderstorm.

Usually, ball lightning appears as a floating, brightly glowing, fuzzy-looking mass that hovers along above the ground. It ranges from the size of a marble to the enormous Widecombe church fireball, but is typically about soccer ball–size. It glows with a white, yellow, orange, or red light, and can last for up to a minute before disappearing with a popping sound or a loud bang. It leaves behind a smell of burning or sulfur—a chemical odor that smells like rotting eggs.

Ball lightning is often described as passing through walls, windows, or even the fuselage of an airplane. In 1963, passengers on a nighttime flight from New York to Washington, D.C., saw ball lightning float along inside the cabin, then disappear at the back of the aircraft. In Sweden in 1944, witnesses saw a glowing, floating ball pass through a glass window, leaving a perfect round hole.

FRIGHT-O-METER
UWILLBE PALLNB
DON'T READ THIS BOOK BEFORE BED
0 1 2 3 4 5 6 7 8 9 10

AN ILLUSTRATION OF RICHMANN'S DISASTROUS EXPERIMENT

BALL LIGHTNING
SCIENCE

UNTIL THE 1960S, MANY PEOPLE, EVEN SCIENTISTS, DIDN'T BELIEVE BALL LIGHTNING WAS A REAL THING. IT WAS SEEN AS AN URBAN LEGEND OR SOMETHING THAT PEOPLE JUST IMAGINED—A LITTLE LIKE GHOSTS OR UFOS. GRADUALLY, THOUGH, MORE AND MORE PEOPLE REPORTED SEEING IT. AS THE RISE OF DIGITAL AND VIDEO CAMERAS MADE IT EASIER TO COLLECT EVIDENCE, IT BECAME CLEAR SOMETHING STRANGE REALLY WAS GOING ON.

SCIENTISTS BEGAN TO LOOK INTO REPORTS OF BALL LIGHTNING AND FOUND THAT IT IS CONNECTED TO THUNDERSTORMS AND SEEMS TO BE CAUSED BY ELECTRICITY IN SOME WAY. HOWEVER, THEY STILL DON'T AGREE ON HOW IT HAPPENS, AND THERE ARE MANY DIFFERENT THEORIES. ONE OF THE PROBLEMS IS THAT BALL LIGHTNING IS SO RARE, IT'S VERY HARD TO GET A CHANCE TO OBSERVE AND STUDY IT.

DON'T TOUCH

Most people who've seen ball lightning have simply watched in amazement as it passed by, and were not harmed. But if the ball does come into contact with you, it can leave you with a burn mark—and in some cases it can be deadly. In 1753, a German scientist, Georg Richmann, was carrying out experiments during a thunderstorm, including flying a kite. A glowing ball seemed to move down the kite string toward him, and hit him on the head, killing him. His shoes were blown off and his clothes were scorched, similar to what can happen when people are struck by normal lightning. The door of the room he was in was also blown off its hinges.

CLOUD-TO-GROUND LIGHTNING STRIKES SOMEWHERE ON EARTH ABOUT **50 TIMES EVERY SECOND,** OR ABOUT 1.5 BILLION TIMES A YEAR!

UNDERGROUND GHOST TOWN

IN EDINBURGH, THE CAPITAL OF SCOTLAND, you can go on a tour to explore a network of ancient underground streets, rooms, and passageways. Known by the name of its main street, Mary King's Close, this is said to be one of Scotland's most haunted places.

DON'T READ THIS BOOK BEFORE BED
0 1 2 3 4 5 6 7 8 9 10
FRIGHT-O-METER
UWILLBUPAL_N8

MEDIEVAL Main Street

"Close" is a Scottish word for a narrow, alley-like street with tall tenements (old-style apartment buildings) on either side. In Edinburgh's old town, the main road, the Royal Mile, runs downhill from the city's cliff-top castle (also said to be haunted). Branching off from it are dozens of closes, built from the 1500s onward, where the city dwellers used to live. Closes were often named after a local trader or shop. Mary King's Close took its name from Mary King, a local seamstress and fabric seller.

Life in MARY KING'S CLOSE

In the 1600s, Mary King's Close and the other closes nearby were normal streets, open to the sky. They were busy and bustling, with lots of homes and shops. But there was one big problem: It stunk. Homes in those days didn't have bathrooms or toilets. People just used bowls called chamber pots instead, and tipped them out into the street!

ANCHOR CLOSE, EDINBURGH, SCOTLAND

CHAMBER POT

In 1645, the plague, or Black Death, ravaged Edinburgh. This deadly disease was spread by fleas on rats, but people didn't realize that at the time. Crowded, dirty living areas, such as the closes, were badly affected. People died in huge numbers.

According to one local legend, the city's leaders, hoping to stop the spread of the plague, bricked up Mary King's Close with the sick and dying left inside. Anyone who didn't get out in time was doomed to die a painful death, with no hope of escape.

Underground GHOULS

After the plague had passed, people went to live in the close again. But there was said to be a horrible infestation—ghosts of the people who had died there! Eventually, the area became run-down and deserted, and in the 1700s, the city demolished some of the tenements around Mary King's Close. A large building called the Royal Exchange was built on top of them, covering them over.

DOCTORS USED TO WEAR SPOOKY MASKS LIKE THIS TO AVOID PLAGUE GERMS.

OTHER SPOOKY SIGHTINGS REPORTED IN MARY KING'S CLOSE INCLUDE STRANGE NOISES AND FOOTSTEPS, GLOWING LIGHTS, THE GHOST OF A DOG WITH NO HEAD, AND AN OLD MAN'S HEAD WITH NO BODY!

IS IT REALLY HAUNTED?

SKEPTICS (PEOPLE WHO DON'T BELIEVE IN THE PARANORMAL) AREN'T CONVINCED BY THESE STORIES. THEY POINT OUT THAT THERE'S NO EVIDENCE THAT THE CLOSE WAS EVER REALLY BRICKED UP TO TRAP PEOPLE INSIDE (ALTHOUGH PEOPLE DEFINITELY DID DIE OF THE PLAGUE THERE). THE AREA WAS NEAR EDINBURGH'S MARSHY NOR LOCH (A LAKE THAT IS NO LONGER THERE). SOME SCIENTISTS THOUGHT GASES ESCAPING FROM THE LOCH COULD CAUSE HALLUCINATIONS, GIVING RISE TO THE GHOST STORIES.

GHOSTLY Girl

Today when you visit Mary King's Close, you'll hear about the many ghosts people say they have spotted there. The most famous is a little girl, aged about eight or nine, known as Annie. The story goes that she was one of the unfortunate people imprisoned in the close during the plague. Some versions say her family lived there, but her parents escaped, leaving her behind. In others, she was simply unlucky enough to be walking through the close when it was shut off.

Now her sad, lonely ghost is said to haunt one of the rooms deep underground. She wanders around, looking for her favorite toy, a lost doll. Some visitors say the room feels cold when you walk into it. Others have reported seeing Annie herself, or feeling a small hand pulling at them. Gulp!

The close, and its rumored ghosts, were left alone for many years. But in 2003, the underground streets were reopened and explored once again. Ghost hunters, history buffs, and spook enthusiasts flocked to the creepy underground town, and it was soon made into a top tourist attraction.

FEELING SORRY FOR ANNIE, VISITORS HAVE LEFT DOLLS, SWEETS, AND OTHER PRESENTS FOR HER IN A CORNER OF THE ROOM, FORMING A KIND OF SPOOKY SHRINE.

ZOMBIE ANTS

IMAGINE YOUR BODY BECAME INFECTED WITH THE SPORES OF A DEADLY FUNGUS. Once inside you, they found their way to your brain, and controlled your behavior, making you head for the nearest tree and climb up to the top. Then they took over your body and killed you, and a ginormous mushroom grew out of your head! Surely that's something that could only happen in a very weird nightmare, or an especially horrible horror movie. But the truth is, it really can happen! To ants, that is.

FRIGHT-O-METER
DON'T READ THIS BOOK BEFORE BED
0 1 2 3 4 5 6 7 8 9 10
UWILLBUPALLN8

FREAKY FUNGUS

A fungus is a type of living thing. Mushrooms, toadstools, molds, and yeasts are all types of fungi. They reproduce by releasing spores, which are a little like seeds, but much smaller. The spores can grow into new fungi.

The killer fungus that attacks ants is the *Cordyceps* fungus. As the ants hurry to and from their nests, they may brush against *Cordyceps* spores on the ground or on plants around them. That's where it starts to get scary! A *Cordyceps* spore can stick to an ant and cling on tightly. Then it releases chemicals that dissolve the surface of the ant's body, so it can burrow inside.

Over the next week or two, the fungus starts to grow and spread through the ant's body, until it reaches its tiny insect brain. There, it releases chemicals that somehow control and change the ant's behavior.

MUST...CLIMB...TREE...

Before it knows what's happening, the ant stops thinking about finding food for its colony, fighting off enemies, or caring for the queen ant. Instead, it gets just one thought in its head—that it must climb up as high as possible. It finds a tree, bush, or other plant, and heads for the top. It has become a "zombie" ant, ruled by the fungus, and unable to think for itself.

Once the ant is as high up as possible, the fungus makes it do something else weird. It bites down on a leaf, keeping its jaws clamped so that it can't fall off. Finally, the ant dies. The freaky fungus then uses it as a food source to grow a mushroomy stalk out of the back of its head.

This part of the fungus is a "fruiting body," similar to a mushroom or toadstool you might see on the ground. As it ripens, it releases many more spores into the air. They float down to the ground, and infect more ants—and so the life cycle of the frightening fungus begins its terrible trek all over again.

ANT WITH A FUNGUS GROWING OUT OF ITS HEAD.

COULD IT HAPPEN TO YOU?

LUCKILY, AS FAR AS WE KNOW, LARGE ANIMALS SUCH AS HUMANS ARE NOT AFFECTED BY ANY TYPE OF *CORDYCEPS* FUNGUS. OTHERWISE, YOU'D SEE ZOMBIE PEOPLE WITH GREAT BIG MUSHROOMS GROWING OUT OF THEIR HEADS.

HOWEVER, THERE IS A PARASITE THAT DOES SEEM TO CHANGE THE WAY HUMANS BEHAVE. IT'S CALLED TOXOPLASMOSIS, OR TOXO, AND PEOPLE CAN CATCH IT FROM UNDERCOOKED MEAT, OR SOMETIMES CAT LITTER TRAYS, AS IT CAN BE CARRIED IN CAT POOP. IT'S VERY COMMON—UP TO A THIRD OF THE PEOPLE IN THE WORLD HAVE BEEN INFECTED WITH IT. IF YOU CATCH TOXO, YOU MIGHT NOT EVEN REALIZE IT, AS IT RARELY MAKES PEOPLE ILL. BUT STUDIES HAVE SHOWN THAT PEOPLE WHO HAVE HAD IT TEND TO BE MORE FRIENDLY AND SOCIABLE, AND MORE LIKELY TO TAKE RISKS. WEIRD!

TOXO ALSO AFFECTS MICE, MAKING THEM LESS SCARED OF CATS—AND MAKING IT EASIER FOR CATS TO CATCH THEM!

SUMMER GRASS, WINTER WORM

There are also other types of *Cordyceps* that affect other creepy-crawlies, such as caterpillars, beetles, or spiders. One type of caterpillar, found in the Himalaya, is known as *yartsa gunbu*, meaning "summer grass, winter worm." In the winter, it's a moth caterpillar (the "worm"), but by the time summer comes, some of the caterpillars can be found with the long, thin fungi (the "grass") growing from their heads.

SUMMER GRASS CATERPILLARS ARE COLLECTED AND SOLD AS MEDICINE.

CREEPY CULLODEN MOOR

IN THE YEAR 1746, A TERRIBLE BATTLE RAGED ACROSS THE MOOR AT CULLODEN, NEAR INVERNESS IN SCOTLAND. Two armies clashed—but they were not evenly matched, and the result was a horrific bloodbath. In less than an hour, more than 1,200 men were gruesomely slaughtered. Do the spirits of those who lost their lives in battle still remain? Some people think so.

FRIGHT-O-METER

KING JAMES STUART

UNFAIR FIGHT

On one side: the Jacobites, followers of King James Stuart, who they saw as the rightful heir to the joint English and Scottish throne. On the other: Britain's powerful government forces, led by merciless Prince William, Duke of Cumberland, son of King George II. His army outnumbered the Jacobites, who were tired after marching for many days. With a combination of gunfire and bayonets, the Jacobites were obliterated. William's men even chased and executed any who managed to escape after the fighting was over.

AN OLD PAINTING OF THE BRUTAL BATTLE

THE DRURY LANE THEATRE IN LONDON, ENGLAND, IS SAID TO HAVE A "RESIDUAL" GHOST, NAMED THE MAN IN GREY.

GHOSTLY ECHOES

Ghosts are often said to haunt places where violent deaths or other traumatic events have taken place. Perhaps that's why Culloden, now a calm, windswept moorland, is home to several spooky specters and ghost sightings.

➔ On the anniversary of the battle, April 16, locals have reported seeing the fighting being replayed in ghostly form. This happened most in the years after the battle, but some say the clashing of swords and the groans of the dying soldiers can still be heard today. There are also reports of sightings of troops of soldiers in the distance, who then disappear ...

➔ Many of the Jacobite army were Scottish Highlanders. After the battle, their bodies were buried in mass graves on the moor. They are still are marked by gravestones for the different Highland clans, or families. According to local tales, birds will not sing around the graves, and heather, a type of flower common on Scottish moors, will not grow there.

➔ The ghost of a tall, stricken-looking Highlander is said to haunt the moor. Those who claim to have seen him say that if you get close enough, you can hear him softly muttering the word "defeated" as he stares at you with his sorrowful eyes ...

➔ In 1936, a visitor lifted up a tartan cloth that had been left on one of the Highlanders' graves. To her horror she saw a vision of a wounded Jacobite soldier lying there—until he vanished!

➔ There's also the super-spooky "Great Scree of Culloden"—an enormous ghostly black bird, said to be a warning of doom, that lurks near the battleground. According to legend, Jacobite soldiers saw the bird the night before the disastrous battle, and several visitors have reported seeing it too.

HAIR-RAISING REPLAY

PARANORMAL RESEARCHERS THEORIZE THAT SOME GHOSTS COULD BE "RECORDED" INTO THEIR SURROUNDINGS, IN THE SAME WAY A VIDEO OR MUSIC IS RECORDED ONTO TAPE OR A COMPUTER CHIP. MANY GHOST REPORTS INVOLVE GHOSTS THAT REPEAT THE SAME ACTION OVER AND OVER, LIKE THE SOLDIERS AT CULLODEN REPLAYING THEIR BATTLE. THEY DON'T SEEM TO SEE ANYONE, OR INTERACT WITH PEOPLE. PEOPLE BELIEVE THAT SOMEHOW, EVENTS FROM THE PAST CAN BE RECORDED INTO THE MATERIALS OF STONES OR WALLS NEARBY. THE RECORDING THEN GETS "REPLAYED" MANY TIMES. THESE GHOSTS ARE SOMETIMES KNOWN AS "RESIDUAL HAUNTINGS," AND THE RECORDING IDEA IS CALLED THE "STONE TAPE THEORY."

THE PROBLEM IS, NO ONE IS YET SURE HOW THIS COULD HAPPEN! THERE'S NO SCIENTIFIC EXPLANATION OF HOW EXACTLY THE RECORDING COULD BE MADE.

MYSTERIOUS MONARCH MIGRATIONS

THINK ABOUT THIS: SOMEWHERE BACK IN THE HISTORY OF YOUR FAMILY TREE, YOU HAVE A GREAT-GRANDMA (YOUR MOTHER'S MOTHER'S MOTHER) WHOM YOU'VE LIKELY NEVER MET. Chances are, she passed away before you were born. You don't know what she looked like, you don't know where she lived, and yet you know that you need to travel to her hometown. No one has given you a map or any information at all. Yet you could set off, somehow sense which town she lived in 3,000 miles (4,828 km) away, find the town, walk down her street, and find her house. Not possible, right? No human could do it. But, guess what—there's one creature on the planet that can: the monarch butterfly.

FRIGHT-O-METER

DON'T READ THIS BOOK BEFORE BED

MILLIONS OF MONARCH BUTTERFLIES CLUSTER TOGETHER IN THE MEXICAN MOUNTAIN FORESTS EVERY WINTER. SOMETIMES THEY COMPLETELY COVER THE TREES!

HIGH AND FLIGHTY

THESE BEAUTIFULLY PATTERNED BLACK-AND-ORANGE BUTTERFLIES MIGRATE ANNUALLY—THEY FLY TO AND FRO BETWEEN CANADA OR THE NORTHEASTERN UNITED STATES FOR THE SUMMER, TO WARMER SOUTHERN CALIFORNIA OR MEXICO FOR THE WINTER.

A monarch that sets off south in the autumn faces a long flight of up to 3,000 miles (4,828 km). It will fly around 50 to 100 miles (80 to 161 km) a day, resting and feeding at night. The whole journey will take several weeks.

That may not sound like much; after all, you may have traveled that distance and more on an airplane. But you weren't using your own body strength—you simply hopped aboard a plane! What a monarch can do is roughly the equivalent of you zooming around the world eight times, simply by flapping your arms!

THERE YET?

THE TRULY MYSTERIOUS AND MIND-BOGGLING PART IS THAT THE BUTTERFLY THAT FLIES HOME TO THE NESTING SITE IS NOT THE SAME BUTTERFLY THAT SET OFF FROM THERE IN THE SPRING. It's actually that butterfly's great-grandchild. And yet it somehow knows exactly where to go.

With birds, fish, whales, and other long-distance migrators, when an animal returns "home," it's returning to the home it came from—or following its parents on the journey to learn the way.

Monarch butterflies are different. Over the course of a year, they go through several life cycles.

MONARCH BUTTERFLY
MIGRATION CYCLE

MONARCH 1: WINTER
- ➲ Spends the winter in the mountains of Mexico, roosting on an oyamel fir tree
- ➲ In March, starts the migration north
- ➲ Along the way, stops to lay eggs, and dies

MONARCH 2: SPRING
- ➲ Continues the migration north
- ➲ Stops and lays its eggs, and dies

MONARCH 3: SUMMER
- ➲ Flies farther north and arrives in Canada
- ➲ Stops to lays its eggs, and dies

MONARCH 4: AUTUMN
- ➲ Lives much longer than the other generations
- ➲ Stores energy
- ➲ Makes the southern migration all the way from Canada to Mexico
- ➲ Returns to the same forest, often to the *exact same tree* as monarch 1 (its great-grandparent!)

MYSTERY SOLVED?

SCIENTISTS STILL DON'T KNOW HOW THE FOURTH-GENERATION MONARCH BUTTERFLY KNOWS HOW TO RETURN TO EXACTLY THE SAME PLACE ITS GREAT-GRANDPARENT SET OUT FROM, BUT THEY HAVE COME UP WITH A FEW THEORIES:

➲ **FOLLOW YOUR NOSE:** Some experts think that as they return south, the monarchs can detect the smell left by the bodies of the butterflies that died on the journey north. Others think maybe the butterflies leave a trail of scent markings on trees and plants, showing later generations the way home. For this to work, the butterflies would need an incredibly good sense of smell, which hasn't been scientifically proven.

➲ **LAY OF THE LAND:** Studies show that on their migrations, monarchs avoid flying over water or high mountains. So it could be that they are forced to follow particular routes, and can't help ending up in roughly the right place. But that still wouldn't explain how they find the exact tree.

➲ **WRITTEN IN THE GENES:** Could monarch butterflies actually have a "map" of where they need to go in their brains, as an instinct inherited from previous generations in their genes? It could be possible, but if so, scientists don't yet know how it works. Maybe it's a combination of all of these—or some other method that we haven't yet discovered.

SCARY SWARMS

MAYBE AT SOME POINT YOU'VE BEEN PINCHED BY A CRAB OR STUNG BY A BEE. It's painful at the time, but nothing you can't handle. Now imagine a SWARM of them, numbering into the hundreds, thousands, or even MILLIONS ... you might rethink going outside for good!

FRIGHT-O-METER
UWILLBUPALLN8
DON'T READ THIS BOOK BEFORE BED
0 1 2 3 4 5 6 7 8 9 10

RED CRAB LARVA ON CHRISTMAS ISLAND

THE CRABS OF CHRISTMAS ISLAND

For some people, just one scuttling crab is enough to scare them off the beach. But millions and millions of them scurrying toward you in a huge swarm? Run for your life! Christmas Island might sound like a joyful holiday getaway, but if you're squeamish about creepy crustaceans, better book your vacation somewhere else!

Meet the Christmas Island red crab—native to this tiny island in the Indian Ocean. For most of the year, the crabs mind their own business—nestled away in the humid rain forest in the middle of the island. They shelter in burrows to stay damp, and feed on leaves and fruit. But come the fall, better put on your boots—the rainy season begins, and so does mating season for the crabs. The problem? They need to lay their eggs in the sea, where they will hatch and the babies will start to grow. So, over a few days, millions of crabs leave the forest, and walk across roads and through towns to get to the seashore.

At times, the crawling, clattering crabs cover the ground completely. People can't help but squash them as they try to walk or drive around. A short hike becomes a recipe for crab soup! The good news is that the people of Christmas Island have found a solution—they've built special underpasses and bridges to help the crabs cross safely, and you keep your boots pinch-free.

SOME TYPES OF MAYFLIES EMERGE IN HUGE SWARMS, BUT LIVE FOR ONLY ONE DAY.

KILLER BEES

Aggressive insects. Widespread attacks. A science experiment gone wrong. A deadly dangerous swarm. This story has all the makings of a horror movie—except it could happen in your own backyard ...

It started in the 1950s, when scientists brought African honeybees to Brazil to try to breed a new type of bee that would make more honey. The African bees tended to be bad-tempered, but they were very productive. By combining them with gentler American bees, scientists hoped to get the best qualities from both types. But the African bees escaped from the labs and naturally bred with local bees. This did NOT work out as planned. It actually created a super-aggressive, incredibly grumpy bee breed. Over time, the new "killer bees" spread across South America, and into parts of North America.

So why are they given the name "killer"? Killer bees don't actually have a worse sting than normal honeybees. The problem is more that they get annoyed so easily. And when they do, the whole colony of bees will swarm, chase, and attack whoever has annoyed them by getting too close to their nest, or even making a loud noise that they didn't like. When this happens, victims can be stung hundreds of times, and that can be deadly, especially if they don't get immediate medical help.

SURVIVING KILLER BEES!

WANT TO KNOW HOW TO STAY SAFE AROUND KILLER BEES? READ ON!

➲ IF KILLER BEES ARE IN THE AREA, AVOID MAKING LOUD NOISES OR VIBRATIONS, OR WEARING STRONG PERFUME. THESE BEES ARE EASILY DISTURBED.

➲ IF KILLER BEES CHASE YOU, RUN. RUN IN A STRAIGHT LINE AND HEAD FOR SHELTER—A BUILDING, CAR, TENT, SHED, OR ANY OTHER SHELTER YOU CAN GET INSIDE AND CLOSE UP. IF THERE'S NO SHELTER, TRY TO CURL UP AND COVER YOURSELF WITH A COAT OR BLANKET.

➲ DON'T SWAT AT THE BEES. IT WILL ONLY MAKE THEM ANGRIER.

➲ DON'T JUMP INTO WATER AND STICK YOUR HEAD UNDER. THE BEES WILL WAIT FOR YOU TO COME UP AND TAKE A BREATH. YIKES!

➲ IF YOU'VE BEEN BADLY STUNG, WAIT UNTIL THE BEES HAVE GONE, THEN GET TO THE HOSPITAL—IMMEDIATELY!

A SWARM OF LOCUSTS!

A SWARM OF LOCUSTS, GRASSHOPPER-LIKE INSECTS THAT LOVE TO EAT FARMERS' CROPS, CAN CONTAIN 10 BILLION INSECTS. IN ONE DAY, THEY CAN EAT 423 MILLION POUNDS (192 MILLION KG) OF PLANTS.

FACELESS GHOSTS

DON'T READ THIS BOOK BEFORE BED

FRIGHT-O-METER
UWILLBUPAL-N8

THE NOPPERA-BO
and the Koi Pond

A long time ago, an old man decided to go fishing for koi carp in the fishponds of the royal palace, because it would be easier than fishing in the river. "You can't do that!" his wife protested. "The palace ponds are sacred and protected by spirits." But the man ignored her, and set off.

On the way, he met his friend, another fisherman, and told him where he was going. "Don't!" his friend warned. "The palace ponds are near a haunted graveyard. It's not safe there." But the man ignored him and went on his way.

As he was about to start fishing in the ponds, a beautiful young woman came up to him. "Please, don't fish in these ponds," she pleaded. He ignored her and took out his fishing gear. Then he looked up and, to his horror, saw the woman's eyes, nose, and mouth fading to nothing, leaving her face smooth, empty, and blank.

In a panic, the man dropped his fishing gear and ran home to his wife. "What's wrong?" his wife asked. "I—I saw a Noppera-bo!" the man wailed. "She came up to me, and then her face disappeared!"

His wife smiled. "Like this, you mean?" she asked, as her features also faded into nothing.

A Tale as OLD AS TIME

If that story sounds familiar, it could be because you've heard something like it in an urban legend or creepy movie. The Noppera-bo originated in Japanese folktales, but people find the faceless ghost so scary, it's been retold and reworked many times, and used in many modern stories too.

ANOTHER MISCHIEVOUS JAPANESE LEGEND CALLED A TENGU IS OFTEN DEPICTED AS A DOG OR CROW.

 to Fright

Although it can scare its victims out of their wits, a Noppera-bo—sometimes known as a mujina—is usually harmless. In most stories it's actually a mischievous ghost that simply enjoys giving people a fright to scare them away from places they're not supposed to be. Often, Noppera-bo seem to work in pairs. The person reports seeing one Noppera-bo, and when they run to tell someone else, it's actually another Noppera-bo pretending to be human!

WHY DO FACES MATTER?

SINCE NOPPERA-BO ARE NOT KNOWN TO HURT PEOPLE, WHY IS THE IDEA OF THEM SO SCARY? RESEARCHERS BELIEVE IT HAS SOMETHING TO DO WITH HOW IMPORTANT FACES ARE TO HUMANS. WE USE FACIAL EXPRESSIONS TO COMMUNICATE. WHEN WE SEE ANOTHER PERSON, WE LOOK AT THEIR FACE FIRST, AS IT'S THE BEST WAY TO TELL HOW THEY ARE FEELING AND WHETHER THEY ARE FRIENDLY. SCIENTISTS HAVE FOUND THAT EVEN IF WE TRY TO FAKE IT, OUR TRUE FEELINGS CAN SHOW ON OUR FACE FOR A SPLIT SECOND—KNOWN AS A "MICRO-EXPRESSION." OTHER PEOPLE CAN OFTEN PICK UP ON THIS.

BY CONTRAST, IF YOU CAN'T SEE SOMEONE'S FACE, IT CAN MAKE YOU FEEL A BIT UNCOMFORTABLE, AS YOU CAN'T "READ" THEIR EMOTIONS. THINK ABOUT MYSTERIOUS VILLAINS IN YOUR FAVORITE MOVIES—OFTENTIMES THEIR FACES ARE FULLY OR PARTIALLY OBSCURED. WHEN A NOPPERA-BO'S FACE DISAPPEARS SUDDENLY, IT GIVES US A SENSE OF PANIC—AS WHAT WE THOUGHT WAS HUMAN BECOMES STRANGE AND SUPERNATURAL.

AS WELL AS APPEARING IN BOOKS AND MOVIES, NOPPERA-BO CHARACTERS HAVE EVEN BEEN MADE INTO (SOMEWHAT TERRIFYING) DOLLS!

Is It REAL?

Noppera-bo are mainly found in stories, and few people claim to have seen a real one. But in Hawaii, which has a large Japanese population, several real-life Noppera-bo sightings have been reported. In 1959, one woman said she had seen a girl combing her red hair in a ladies' restroom. As she approached, the girl turned to face her—but had no face!

Japanese

The Noppera-bo is one Japan's many *yokai*—the name for things that are paranormal, unexplained, supernatural, ghostly, weird, or creepy. There are many Japanese folktales about different kinds of yokai, and real-life reports of yokai sightings too. In fact, most of the creepy things in this book could be described as yokai.

"THE NIGHT PARADE OF ONE HUNDRED DEMONS" BY ARTIST KAWANABE KYOSAI

QUIZ

ARE YOU AFRAID OF THE DARK?

MOST PEOPLE WILL PROBABLY FIND SOMETHING IN THIS BOOK THAT REALLY SCARES THE PANTS OFF THEM, but we're all different. Some people are terrified of creepy-crawlies and bugs; others will happily pick up a spider, but won't sleep in the dark in case a monster grabs their foot! Follow our frightful flowchart quiz to see where your deepest fears lie ...

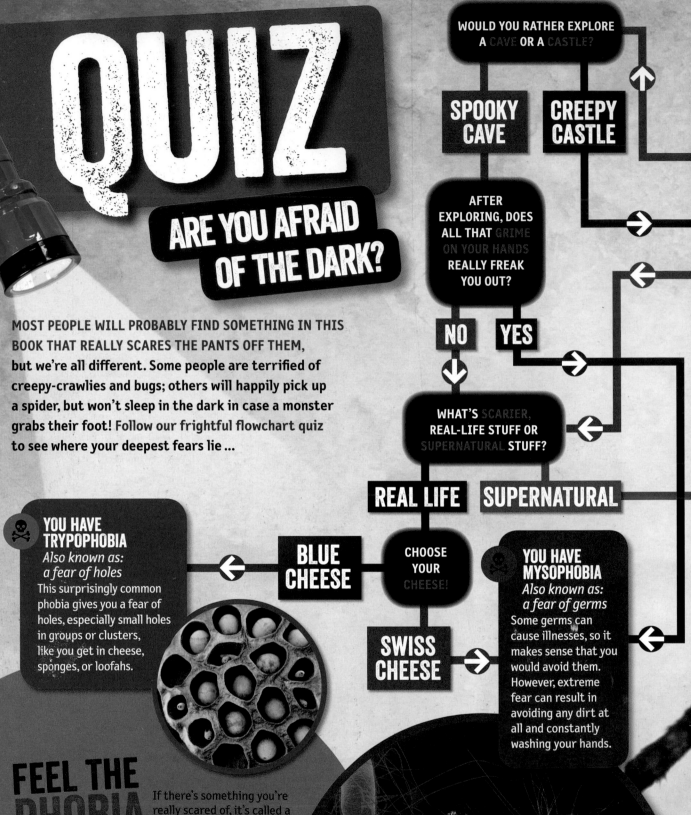

WOULD YOU RATHER EXPLORE A CAVE OR A CASTLE?

SPOOKY CAVE | CREEPY CASTLE

AFTER EXPLORING, DOES ALL THAT GRIME ON YOUR HANDS REALLY FREAK YOU OUT?

NO | YES

WHAT'S SCARIER, REAL-LIFE STUFF OR SUPERNATURAL STUFF?

REAL LIFE | SUPERNATURAL

CHOOSE YOUR CHEESE!

BLUE CHEESE

SWISS CHEESE

☠ YOU HAVE TRYPOPHOBIA
Also known as: a fear of holes
This surprisingly common phobia gives you a fear of holes, especially small holes in groups or clusters, like you get in cheese, sponges, or loofahs.

☠ YOU HAVE MYSOPHOBIA
Also known as: a fear of germs
Some germs can cause illnesses, so it makes sense that you would avoid them. However, extreme fear can result in avoiding any dirt at all and constantly washing your hands.

FEEL THE PHOBIA
If there's something you're really scared of, it's called a phobia. Phobias range from things that most people find a bit scary, like being high up, to things that are very unlikely to hurt you, such as baked beans. Phobias often have interesting names, like the ones on these pages.

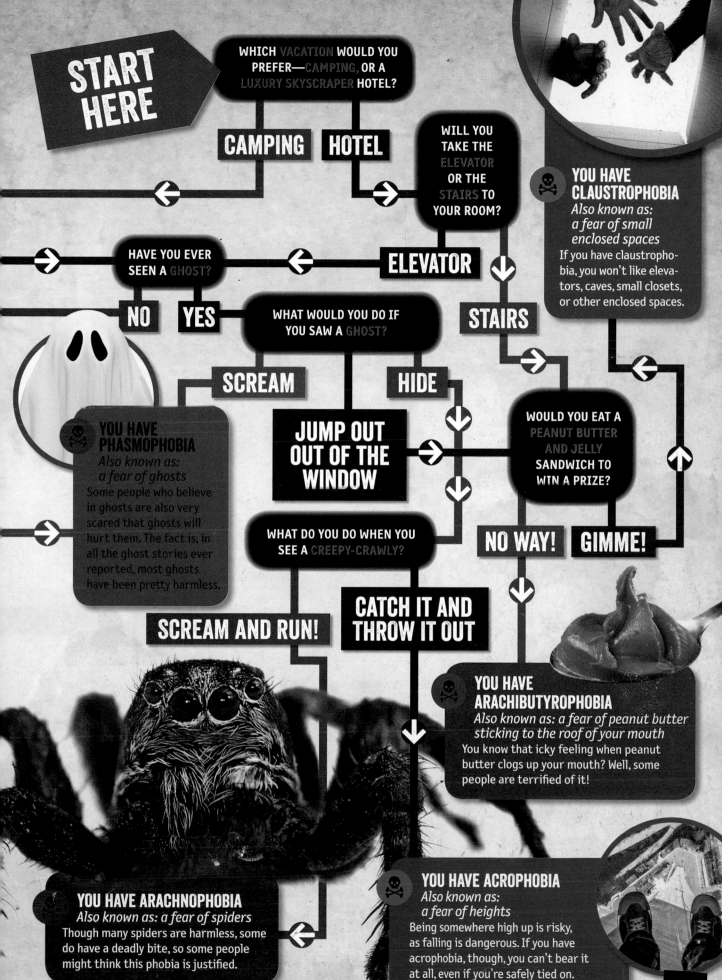

START HERE

WHICH VACATION WOULD YOU PREFER—CAMPING, OR A LUXURY SKYSCRAPER HOTEL?

CAMPING   **HOTEL**

WILL YOU TAKE THE ELEVATOR OR THE STAIRS TO YOUR ROOM?

YOU HAVE CLAUSTROPHOBIA
Also known as: a fear of small enclosed spaces
If you have claustrophobia, you won't like elevators, caves, small closets, or other enclosed spaces.

HAVE YOU EVER SEEN A GHOST?

ELEVATOR

NO   **YES**

WHAT WOULD YOU DO IF YOU SAW A GHOST?

STAIRS

SCREAM   **HIDE**

YOU HAVE PHASMOPHOBIA
Also known as: a fear of ghosts
Some people who believe in ghosts are also very scared that ghosts will hurt them. The fact is, in all the ghost stories ever reported, most ghosts have been pretty harmless.

JUMP OUT OUT OF THE WINDOW

WOULD YOU EAT A PEANUT BUTTER AND JELLY SANDWICH TO WIN A PRIZE?

WHAT DO YOU DO WHEN YOU SEE A CREEPY-CRAWLY?

NO WAY!   **GIMME!**

SCREAM AND RUN!   **CATCH IT AND THROW IT OUT**

YOU HAVE ARACHIBUTYROPHOBIA
Also known as: a fear of peanut butter sticking to the roof of your mouth
You know that icky feeling when peanut butter clogs up your mouth? Well, some people are terrified of it!

YOU HAVE ARACHNOPHOBIA
Also known as: a fear of spiders
Though many spiders are harmless, some do have a deadly bite, so some people might think this phobia is justified.

YOU HAVE ACROPHOBIA
Also known as: a fear of heights
Being somewhere high up is risky, as falling is dangerous. If you have acrophobia, though, you can't bear it at all, even if you're safely tied on.

BLAST INTO THE PAST

FRIGHT-O-METER

DON'T READ THIS BOOK BEFORE BED

0 1 2 3 4 5 6 7 8 9 10

UWILL TUPALLN8

IN SCI-FI BOOKS AND MOVIES, PEOPLE CAN SIMPLY CLIMB INTO A MACHINE AND TRAVEL TO A PREDETERMINED DESTINA-TION IN TIME. In real life, we still haven't quite figured out time travel yet. Many scientists think it is possible—the late great Albert Einstein proved that time can travel at different speeds, and that by zooming incredibly fast, you can actually slow time down, if only very slightly. But how to turn that information into a seat at a Roman banquet or sitting in the cheering section at a medieval tournament? Is it really possible?

THE GHOSTS OF **PETIT TRIANON**

LOST IN **TIME**

THERE ARE SOME PEOPLE WHO HAVE DESCRIBED HAVING WEIRD EXPERI-ENCES EXACTLY LIKE THAT—SUDDENLY FINDING THEMSELVES IN THE MIDDLE OF A SCENE FROM THE PAST. But instead of climbing aboard a time machine and going there on purpose, it seems to happen randomly and by accident. One of the most famous cases happened in France, at a fabulous and famous palace.

IN 1901, TWO UNIVERSITY TEACHERS FROM OXFORD, ENGLAND, CHARLOTTE ANNE MOBERLY AND ELEANOR JOURDAIN, WENT ON A TRIP TO PARIS, THE CAPITAL OF FRANCE. During their stay, the women decided to visit Versailles—a huge royal palace and garden complex where the French king Louis XVI and his wife, Marie Antoinette, lived in the lap of luxury in the 1700s. They were famed for their extravagant lifestyle of glamorous parties, expensive clothes, and countless servants.

After visiting the main palace, Moberly and Jourdain went to look for the Petit Trianon, a smaller house that was Queen Marie Antoinette's private residence. It was about a mile (1.6 km) from the main palace, hidden away in the vast gardens of Versailles.

And that's when things got weird. As they described it later, the friends got very lost, and began to see a series of odd, old-fashioned buildings, and people—and perhaps even Marie Antoinette herself!

HOUSE IN THE VILLAGE OF TRIANON, VERSAILLES

SPOOKY **SIGHTS**

- ➲ First, Moberly saw a small, old-looking stone cottage and a woman shaking a cloth out the window. Jourdain saw what looked like a ruined farmhouse, with an old plow and farm equipment. They hadn't noticed anything like this before on the otherwise luxuriously manicured estate.

- ➲ They both felt that the atmosphere changed, and they were overwhelmed with a feeling of sadness.

- ➲ They met two men in strange, long green coats and tricornered hats. The men told them to keep walking straight on.

- ➲ Jourdain saw another ancient cottage, with a woman and a girl in old-fashioned clothes in the doorway. She described them as seeming to be stuck in time, like a waxwork.

- ➲ Moberly later recalled that the trees and landscape looked flat, still, and unreal.

- ➲ They came across a man sitting in a garden, wearing a large hat and cloak, his dark face marked with smallpox. The two women immediately felt afraid and walked away.

- ➲ Another, taller, curly-haired man with a wide-brimmed hat and historical clothes appeared and directed them to the Petit Trianon. To get there, they crossed a small bridge.

- ➲ When they arrived at the Petit Trianon gardens, Moberly saw a fair-haired woman in an elegant, old-fashioned dress, sitting on the lawn and sketching.

The eerie encounter ended when they bumped into some other tourists, and suddenly everything was back to normal.

The women came to the conclusion that they had seen Versailles as it was in 1789, just before the French Revolution that toppled Louis XVI and Marie Antoinette. In 1911, they published a book about their experience, *An Adventure*, which became a best seller.

SPOOKY TIME SLIPS

COULD THIS KIND OF THING REALLY HAPPEN? MAYBE MOBERLY AND JOURDAIN DIDN'T ACTUALLY TIME TRAVEL, BUT SOMEHOW SAW A REPLAY OF A DAY FROM THE PAST—SIMILAR TO A "RECORDED" GHOST (SEE PAGE 59). A FEW OTHER PEOPLE HAVE REPORTED SIMILAR EXPERIENCES, WHICH ARE KNOWN AS "TIME SLIPS."

ONE SUCH STORY DATES FROM 1996 IN LIVERPOOL, ENGLAND. A COUPLE WENT SHOPPING IN THE CITY AND HEADED OFF TO VISIT SEPARATE SHOPS. WHEN THE MAN WENT TO REJOIN HIS WIFE, HE WAS AMAZED TO SEE THE BOOKSHOP SHE HAD GONE TO HAD DIS-APPEARED, AND AN OLD-FASHIONED SHOP WITH A DIFFERENT NAME STOOD IN ITS PLACE. HE LOOKED AROUND AND SAW VANS AND CARS FROM THE 1950S ON THE STREET. PEOPLE WERE WEARING OLD-FASHIONED OUTFITS. AS HE APPROACHED THE SHOP, THE MAN SAW THAT IT SOLD CLOTHES AND UMBRELLAS. HE WENT INSIDE— AND FOUND HIMSELF IN THE MODERN BOOKSHOP AFTER ALL. WEIRD!

FACT OR **FICTION?**

WHILE MANY PEOPLE READ THE BOOK, QUITE A FEW DID NOT BELIEVE IT. They thought the women must have imagined it, or made up the story to make money.

To this day, there is no clear explanation for what happened. Some people think the friends got lost and confused, and encouraged each other to believe they had traveled in time. Others have suggested that what they actually saw was a fancy-dress party thrown by the poet and art collector Robert de Montesquiou, who lived nearby. The two women passed away nearly 100 years ago, so we may never know what they truly experienced that day.

THE INFINITE MULTIVERSE

FRIGHT-O-METER
DON'T READ THIS BOOK BEFORE BED
0 1 2 3 4 5 6 7 8 9 10
UWILLBLPALLN8

WHAT ARE YOU DOING RIGHT NOW? READING, TAPPING YOUR FOOT, WEARING YOUR FAVORITE JEANS, EATING A SNACK ... PROBABLY A NUMBER OF THINGS. But what if you weren't the only "you" out there? What if there were countless other yous, all doing different things, somewhere far away? Welcome to the weird world of the multiverse!

Unlike some of the spooky topics in this book, the multiverse isn't something paranormal or supernatural, like a ghost or a vampire. It's actually a serious explanation for how the universe might really work, according to physicists. However, not all scientists agree about it, and no one can be sure if it's true.

THE FARTHEST REACHES

"Universe" is a word scientists use to mean everything there is—or everything we can see around us, both here on Earth and when we look out into space with telescopes, as well as things far beyond our field of vision. That means all the stars, planets, moons, black holes, and galaxies in space (not to mention all of the empty space in between).

However, it's hard to say exactly how big the universe is, and what it's like, as we can't see far enough to tell. Does the universe have an "edge"? Is it possible to go outside the universe? If it is, what happens there? Scientists aren't sure, but they try to come up with ideas or theories to answer these questions.

SOME SCIENTISTS BELIEVE OUR UNIVERSE COULD BE SHAPED LIKE A DOUGHNUT, AS SEEN IN THIS COMPUTER ARTWORK.

AND BEYOND

One of these theories is the idea of a multiverse, or many universes, all existing at the same time. According to some scientists, it's very unlikely that our universe could exist on its own. The way the stars and planets are arranged, the course of history, and all the decisions we make, happen in one particular way. And the chances of it happening exactly that way are very tiny!

But if there are countless other universes, that would make more sense. In each of these other universes, things happen slightly differently—or very differently. Every time something happens, it's happening in other ways too, in an infinite, or endless, number of other universes. If everything is happening somewhere, then it's not so unlikely. Simple, right? Or not so much ...

SCIENTISTS ESTIMATE THERE ARE AT LEAST A TRILLION TRILLION (THAT'S 1,000,000,000, 000,000,000,000,000) STARS IN OUR UNIVERSE.

THE YOUS YOU DON'T KNOW

That would mean that if you decided to have a cheese sandwich yesterday, another you, somewhere in a different universe, had a peanut butter sandwich. Another you would have chosen a hamburger instead. There would also be universes where you were taller or shorter, or had a different name, or never even existed. There would be universes where no one existed, or there were other, alien life-forms, or octopuses ruled the world. In the multiverse theory, anything that can happen, does happen—somewhere out there.

DON'T PANIC

It's kind of fun—or scary—to imagine there are other "yous" in other universes. Would all of the yous like the same food? Listen to the same music? Look like you? It's pretty mind-boggling to think about—but it is just a theory. We can't test it to see if it's true, because we could never reach the other universes. So don't lie awake at night wondering what the other yous are up to! You'll never meet them (if they exist), so it doesn't really matter after all.

OUR UNIVERSE IS PROBABLY ABOUT 13.8 BILLION YEARS OLD.

WHERE IN THE WORLD?

IF ALL THESE OTHER UNIVERSES EXIST, WHERE ARE THEY? WELL, SCIENTISTS HAVE SEVERAL DIFFERENT IDEAS ABOUT THIS.

➔ THE PATCHWORK QUILT
SOME SAY ALL THE UNIVERSES ARE SPREAD OUT NEXT TO EACH OTHER, STRETCHING OFF IN ALL DIRECTIONS, LIKE A PATCHWORK QUILT.

➔ BUBBLE UNIVERSES
ACCORDING TO THIS IDEA, THE UNIVERSES ARE ALL SEPARATE, LIKE BUBBLES FLOATING AROUND IN AN INFINITELY LARGE SPACE.

➔ PARALLEL UNIVERSES
IN THIS THEORY, ALL THE UNIVERSES EXIST IN THE SAME SPACE AND AT THE SAME TIME, BUT IN DIFFERENT DIMENSIONS. WE CAN'T ACCESS THEM OR MOVE BETWEEN THEM, BECAUSE ALL THE UNIVERSES EXIST IN DIFFERENT WAYS OR ON DIFFERENT "LEVELS."

COMPUTER ARTWORK OF BUBBLE UNIVERSES

BLOODSUCKING BATS

DON'T READ THIS BOOK BEFORE BED

0 1 2 3 4 5 6 7 8 9 10

FRIGHT-O-METER

UWILLBUPALLN8

A VAMPIRE, AS YOU KNOW BY NOW, IS AN UNDEAD GHOUL THAT CREEPS AROUND IN THE NIGHT, BITING PEOPLE ON THE NECK AND SLURPING UP THEIR BLOOD. Luckily, though books and movies are full of them, there's not much evidence that real vampires exist. But vampire bats ARE real, and they really do drink human blood! So cover your neck and prepare to be terrified: Vampire bats might be coming for you!

A VAMPIRE BAT FINDS A GOOD PLACE TO BITE.

BLOOD FOR LUNCH

First, the good news: Vampire bats only live in South and Central America. They aren't big—in fact, compared to other bats, they are quite tiny. A vampire bat could sit in your hand, and weighs less than an apple. And they generally don't bite humans. There are three types, or species, of vampire bat. The hairy-legged vampire bat and the white-winged vampire bat both prefer sucking the blood of birds. Now the bad news: The third species, the common vampire bat, is the one that might decide to bite you, as it's good at moving around close to the ground, where humans are more likely to sleep. But even then, it's more likely to sink its teeth into a cow or a pig.

A VAMPIRE BAT CAN SPRING UP TO **THREE FEET (1 M)** INTO THE **AIR.**

DINNER
IS SERVED

If you are unlucky enough to be bitten by a vampire bat, here's what will happen. In the night, as you sleep, the bat will fly in (maybe you shouldn't have left that window open!) and land a little distance away. Then, to approach you as quietly as possible, it will tiptoe along the ground, using its folded wings as front "feet."

Then, the bat will use a special heat sensor on its nose to detect which bits of your skin are warmest. This reveals where blood vessels run closest to the skin surface. Using its razor-sharp fangs, it will make a small cut in the skin, so that the blood runs out. The bat laps up the blood with its tongue, rather than actually sucking it out. Its saliva contains chemicals that stop the blood from clotting, and keep it nice and runny. Finally, the bat will walk away full and happy, leap into the air, and fly off into the night.

SUPERSHARP
INCISORS

Pretty terrifying, right? Fortunately, if a vampire bat decides you'd make a nice feast, you're unlikely to even wake up. That's because its teeth are so sharp, you don't even feel them slicing into your skin! Scientists who are handling dead vampire bats, or even vampire bat skeletons, still have to be careful, as the incredibly sharp front teeth can easily cut them.

However, it's still best to avoid being bitten by a vampire bat if you can. Their bites can sometimes spread bugs and diseases.

HUNGRY FOR
HEMOGLOBIN

VAMPIRE BATS AREN'T THE ONLY ANIMALS THAT LIKE TO OF COURSE, MANY INSECTS DO IT—INCLUDING MOSQUITOES, BITING MIDGES, BEDBUGS, AND FLEAS. SO DO SOME TYPES OF LEECHES—WORMLIKE ANIMALS THAT LIVE IN PONDS AND STREAMS. THEY TO THEIR PREY TO SUCK OUT BLOOD, AND THEY CAN BE HARD TO PULL OFF. THERE ARE EVEN BIRDS THAT SUCK BLOOD, LIKE THE VAMPIRE FINCH OF THE GALÁPAGOS ISLANDS. THIS MINI MONSTER WILL PECK LARGER BIRDS UNTIL THEY BLEED, AND FEED ON THE BLOOD. AND IN CASE YOU THINK THESE CALLOUS CREATURES SHOULD BE EXTERMINATED, KEEP THIS IN MIND: A BLOOD PUDDING OR BLOOD SAUSAGE IS A FOOD MADE OF BLOOD MIXED WITH FAT AND OATS OR OTHER INGREDIENTS, AND COOKED UNTIL IT TURNS SOLID. ALMOST EVERY COUNTRY HAS ITS OWN RECIPE. AND AMONG THE CATTLE-FARMING MAASAI PEOPLE OF EAST AFRICA, COWS' BLOOD MIXED WITH COWS' MILK IS A TRADITIONAL DRINK.

THE TERRIFYING TOWER

THE TOWER OF LONDON IS SAID TO BE ONE OF THE WORLD'S MOST HAUNTED BUILDINGS. A 900-year-old castle in the middle of London, England's capital city, it has a long history of terror, torture, murder, and misery. Not to mention a seriously scary selection of spooks!

DON'T READ THIS BOOK BEFORE BED

0 1 2 3 4 5 6 7 8 9 10

FRIGHT-O-METER

UWILLBUPAL_N8

HISTORIC ILLUSTRATION OF THE TOWER OF LONDON

HARROWING History

Since the construction of the oldest parts of the Tower of London in 1078, it has had a variety of different uses. It's been a royal residence; an armory, or arsenal (where weapons were stored); a treasure storehouse; a mint (where money was made); and even a royal menagerie, or zoo!

But most infamously of all, it was used as a prison where kings and queens would lock up their archenemies. And quite a few people have been brutally executed or murdered within its walls, or on Tower Hill nearby. Famously grumpy English king Henry VIII, who ruled in the 1500s, was notorious for sending people who had annoyed him to the Tower—including two of his own wives!—and then having them publicly beheaded for their crimes.

So if you'd like to see some spooky sights, the Tower of London is the place to go. Here are just a few of the ghoulish ghosts that have been spotted there ...

THE TOWER OF LONDON IS FAMOUS FOR THE BIG, BLACK RAVENS, A TYPE OF BIRD, THAT LIVE THERE. ACCORDING TO LEGEND, IF THEY EVER LEAVE, THE TOWER WILL FALL DOWN.

THE HEADLESS Ghost

Anne Boleyn was the second of Henry VIII's six wives, but he wanted her out of his way after she failed to give him a son. (In those days, kings thought you needed a son to rule after you died—but tell that to Queen Elizabeth I, Henry's daughter and one of the greatest monarchs in history!) He accused Anne of betraying him and had her locked up in the Tower, then sent to the guillotine where she was beheaded! Anne's ghost is said to appear outside the chapel, where her execution took place. She is said to be missing her head, but sometimes carries it in her arms.

ANNE BOLEYN

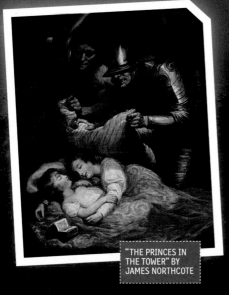
"THE PRINCES IN THE TOWER" BY JAMES NORTHCOTE

The Princes IN THE TOWER

In 1483, King Edward IV died, making his 12-year-old son, Edward V, the next king. But Richard, the dead king's brother, wanted the throne for himself. Since the new king was still a child, Richard was named his protector and charged with looking after Edward and his nine-year-old brother until Edward was old enough to rule. Instead, under the pretense that he was protecting them, Richard sent the boys to live in the Tower of London. Soon after, the princes disappeared and Richard himself grabbed the throne. It's believed that he murdered the boys, or had them murdered—and in 1674, workmen found two small skeletons buried near the White Tower. People have reported seeing the two boys' ghosts, and hearing them laughing and playing.

The Gruesome EXECUTION

Margaret Pole was another victim of cruel King Henry VIII. Her son had offended the king, but he was not in the country at the time, so Henry imprisoned Margaret instead, although she was an innocent old lady. After spending more than two years in the Tower, Margaret was taken out to be beheaded. According to legend, she refused to put her head on the chopping block, and ran away, yelling that she was not a traitor. Not to be outdone, the executioner chased her around Tower Green, striking her with an ax. People have reported seeing this gruesome event replaying itself in ghostly form.

MARGARET POLE TRIES TO AVOID A GRUESOME END.

THE Animal Apparition

In 1816, a Tower guard had a good scare when he suddenly saw a huge bear lumbering toward him. He tried to stab it with his bayonet, but to his horror his weapon went harmlessly right through it—the bear was a ghost! The man is said to have died of shock a few days later.

EERIE EVEREST

EVERYONE'S HEARD OF HAUNTED HOUSES AND CASTLES ... BUT HAUNTED MOUNTAINS? Now that's a good ghost story. But according to some brave souls, it's true. The highest mountain in the world, Mount Everest, is a pretty spooky place. Its steepest slopes are often shrouded in cloud cover, and the dangers of freezing temperatures, dizzying altitude, and the possibility of powerful avalanches are enough to drive away all but the most danger-seeking daredevils. Few go up, and even fewer come down. In fact, the monster mountain is actually scattered with the bodies of climbers who have died while trying to scale the peak. No wonder several people have reported feeling a ghostly presence there!

DON'T READ THIS BOOK BEFORE BED

0 1 2 3 4 5 6 7 8 9 10

FRIGHT-O-METER

UWILLBUPALLN8

OF ALL THE PEOPLE ON EARTH, JUST A FEW THOUSAND HAVE BEEN TO THE TOP OF MOUNT EVEREST. SEVERAL HUNDRED ATTEMPT THE CLIMB EACH YEAR, BUT MANY OF THEM HAVE TO TURN BACK IN BAD WEATHER.

SHERPAS PASS A PILE OF ROCKS WHILE CARRYING THEIR HEAVY LOADS.

THE DISAPPEARING DUO

Mountaineer Andrew Irvine made an early attempt to conquer Mount Everest in the year 1924, along with his climbing partner George Mallory. The men made good progress, and were seen making it almost to the top. But then they disappeared, and did not return to their camp lower down the mountain.

No one can be sure if they did actually make it to the summit, and died on the way back, or never quite reached the peak. Their bodies lay undiscovered on Mount Everest for decades. In 1999, George Mallory's body was finally found, but Irvine's is still out there, although a Chinese climber named Wang Hongbao claimed to have spotted it.

GEORGE MALLORY IN 1909

HELPFUL HAUNTING

Since he died at age 22, Andrew Irvine's ghost is said to haunt the mountain, although not in a scary way. Instead, climbers who are struggling say they have sensed him accompanying them, urging them on and encouraging them.

In 1975, two climbers, Doug Scott and Douglas Halston, claim to have felt an invisible presence join them and comfort them as they spent a freezing night in a snow hole near Everest's summit. In the same year, another climber, Nick Estcourt, described an incident in which he was climbing alone up a slope when he saw another climber on the rope below him. He waited, but the other climber slowed down. Eventually, Estcourt decided to keep going—and the climber below him disappeared.

MOUNT EVEREST IS 29,035 FEET (8,850 M) TALL—THE SUMMIT IS ABOUT AS HIGH AS AN AIRPLANE FLIES WHILE AT CRUISING ALTITUDE.

ICY GRAVES

SADLY, MANY PEOPLE WHO TRY TO CLIMB MOUNT EVEREST DIE IN THE ATTEMPT, EITHER ON THE WAY UP, OR CLIMBING BACK DOWN. OFTEN, ESPECIALLY IF THEY ARE IN A VERY HIGH OR HARD-TO-REACH PLACE, THEIR BODIES ARE DIFFICULT TO REMOVE— SO THEY STAY WHERE THEY ARE. IT'S SO COLD, THE BODIES ARE PRESERVED AND DO NOT ROT AWAY. IN OTHER WORDS, EVERY CLIMBER WHO MAKES THEIR WAY UP AND DOWN THE MOUNTAIN IS REMINDED HOW DANGEROUS IT IS, AS THEY LITERALLY PASS BY THE BODIES OF THOSE WHO DID NOT MAKE IT. SOME BODIES ARE RETRIEVED, BUT THIS IS A TRICKY TASK, OFTEN INVOLVING A WHOLE TEAM OF CLIMBERS. OTHERS, SUCH AS THE BODY OF GEORGE MALLORY, HAVE BEEN BURIED IN THE SPOT WHERE THEY WERE FOUND. CLIMBERS SOMETIMES PILE STONES AROUND THE BODIES THEY FIND, OR COVER THEM WITH A BLANKET OR FLAG.

EACH TIME SOMEONE TRIES TO CLIMB EVEREST, THEY HAVE ROUGHLY A 1 IN 20 CHANCE OF DYING IN THE ATTEMPT.

SPIRITS OF THE DEAD

When thrill-seeking tourists decide to scale the world's highest summit, they often hire local mountain people, called Sherpas, as guides and porters to help them reach the top. To the Sherpas, who make their living on the mountain, Everest is known as Chomolungma, meaning "Goddess Mother of the Earth," and in their traditional folklore, it is a sacred place where spirits live.

In 2004, after climbing the mountain, a Sherpa named Pemba Dorje described how he had seen dark shadowy shapes near the top. He believed they were the spirits of the many mountaineers who have died there, and whose bodies have not been recovered or properly buried.

ABANDONED CITY

APRIL 26, 1986, IS A DATE THE WORLD WILL NEVER FORGET. During a routine test at Chernobyl, a huge power plant in Russia, a sudden power surge blew up a nuclear reactor and started an uncontrollable fire. Radioactive smoke churned into the sky and spread over a wide area, posing a deadly danger to wildlife, plants, and people.

DON'T READ THIS BOOK BEFORE BED

0 1 2 3 4 5 6 7 8 9 10

FRIGHT-O-METER

UWILLBUFALLN8

EVERYBODY OUT!

Two miles (3 km) away stood Pripyat, a city of almost 50,000 people, where most of the workers at the nuclear plant lived with their families. The accident happened during the night, at about 1:30 a.m. local time—and the people of Pripyat woke up to find their town in chaos. Some curious locals ventured closer to the power station to get a good look. But by the next day, the government had decided to evacuate everyone from the area, because of the risk of radioactive fallout.

The authorities arranged for more than a thousand buses to rush everyone in the town away to safety. People did not think they would be gone for long. They were told they would be able to return home once the danger had passed, and the nuclear plant had been cleaned up. So, over the course of just a few hours, everyone rushed to collect their families and get out of town, leaving most of their worldly possessions behind.

But before too long, it became clear the information they had been given was wrong. In fact, the destruction of the meltdown was devastating. Pripyat was so badly contaminated with nuclear waste, it would not be safe for people to return to their homes for 24,000 years!

СТІЙ!
ЗАБОРОНЕНА ЗОНА

100 YEARS AGO

IN COLORADO, U.S.A., WAS A BUSY GOLD AND SILVER MINING TOWN. WHEN THE

SO DID THE PEOPLE,

GONE AND FORGOTTEN

Imagine having to board a bus with no notice, leaving behind your home, your school, the familiar streets and buildings, and everything you owned. If you'd known, you would have probably grabbed a few of the things you hold most dear. But the people of Pripyat did not get the chance. All of their food, furniture, machines, books, toys, and other belongings stayed just as they had been left, in the middle of being used, worked on, or played with. Over time, they began to decay, rust, and collapse. Homes became overgrown with moss and mold, and covered in dust and cobwebs. The town's Ferris wheel, stopped forever, stood as a lonely symbol of the busy, happy town Pripyat had once been. Though it's not safe to live there, some former residents have been back to pay a last visit to their old homes, but they still cannot retrieve any of their contaminated possessions. The only other visitors have been reporters and photographers who want to capture the spooky abandoned city on camera.

VAROSHA, IN CYPRUS, IS AN ABANDONED SEASIDE RESORT. IT WAS EVACUATED DURING A TURKISH INVASION IN 1974, AND HAS BEEN EMPTY EVER SINCE.

A RETURN TO NATURE

The scenes at Pripyat show what happens to a city when the people leave it behind. Humans work non-stop to clean, maintain, and tidy our cities. We pull out weeds, clean up bird poop, and wash away mud and bugs from our homes. When no one does that, soil, seeds, and plants start to make their way back in, and eventually take over. One day, it will be hard to tell humans lived here at all!

A FERRIS WHEEL AT THE CENTER OF PRIPYAT THAT NEVER HAD A CHANCE TO OPEN

WHY IS RADIATION DANGEROUS?

NUCLEAR POWER PLANTS WORK BY SPLITTING APART ATOMS, THE TINY UNITS THAT ALL MATTER IS MADE OF, WHICH RELEASES A HUGE AMOUNT OF ENERGY. IN ORDER TO DO THIS, SCIENTISTS USE DANGEROUS, RADIOACTIVE MATERIALS CALLED URANIUM AND PLUTONIUM. WE USE THIS NUCLEAR POWER TO GENERATE ELECTRICITY.

AFTER THEY HAVE BEEN USED TO MAKE NUCLEAR ENERGY, THESE MATERIALS PRODUCE NUCLEAR WASTE, WHICH IS ALSO RADIOACTIVE. RADIOACTIVE SUBSTANCES ARE DANGEROUS TO HUMANS BECAUSE THEY RELEASE TINY PARTICLES OR RAYS OF ENERGY THAT CAN HARM LIVING CELLS. A HIGH DOSE OF RADIATION CAN BE DEADLY. A LOWER DOSE CAN AFFECT THE BODY MORE GRADUALLY, CAUSING SOME TYPES OF ILLNESSES, SUCH AS CANCER, OVER TIME.

WHEN A NUCLEAR POWER PLANT IS WORKING PROPERLY, THE RADIOACTIVE SUBSTANCES ARE ENCLOSED AND KEPT SAFE. BUT AN EXPLOSION LIKE THE ONE IN 1986 CAN RELEASE THEM INTO THE AIR AND SPREAD THEM OVER A WIDE AREA. BECAUSE OF THE RADIOACTIVE WASTE AND THE RISK OF ACCIDENTS, NUCLEAR POWER IS NOT A PERFECT SOLUTION. SCIENTISTS ARE WORKING ON NEWER, SAFER WAYS OF MAKING ELECTRICITY BY HARNESSING NATURAL RESOURCES LIKE THE SUN, WIND, AND WATER.

QUIZ
SPOT THE FAKE PHOTOS

PHOTO 1

HUMP OF LOCH NESS MONSTER, 2012

Seasoned Nessie-watcher and cruise boat captain George Edwards released this photo in 2012. It seems to show the hump of the Loch Ness monster rising above the water.

◻ FAKE ◻ UNEXPLAINED

IT ISN'T ALWAYS EASY TO CATCH A GHOST, monster, or UFO on camera. They tend to make fleeting appearances, and often disappear after a few seconds. And people who claim to have seen ghosts say that cameras and other electrical equipment often seem to stop working, or run out of battery power, during the haunting.

But there are quite a few ghostly and spooky images on the Internet. The question is, which ones really do seem to show something mysterious—and which ones were faked? Can you identify the lies in the pictures on these page?

1

BUT IS IT REAL? *Of course, the fact that a photo is unexplained doesn't mean that it really does show something paranormal. It could just be that it's a very good fake that no one has fessed up to yet! Or it could be a trick of the light, something going wrong with the camera, or a photo of something else, such as an aircraft or an animal that happens to look weird and spooky. That doesn't stop some of these pictures from being pretty unnerving, though!*

PHOTO 2

FACES IN THE WAVES, 1924

In 1924, two sailors on board the S.S. *Watertown* died from inhaling fumes while cleaning out a tank. Over the next few days, the crew reported seeing the men's faces in the waves, following the ship. The captain took several photos of them, and this is the most famous.

◻ FAKE ◻ UNEXPLAINED

2

PHOTO 3
WEM TOWN HALL GHOST, 1995

This famously scary photo, taken by an amateur photographer, shows a town hall being destroyed by fire. When the picture was developed, it showed a girl standing calmly among the flames.

☐ **FAKE** ☐ **UNEXPLAINED**

PHOTO 4
McMINNVILLE UFO, 1950

Evelyn and Paul Trent described how they had spotted a UFO from their farm near McMinnville, Oregon, U.S.A., and had managed to take two photos of it.

☐ **FAKE** ☐ **UNEXPLAINED**

4

PHOTO 5
FILM OF A BIGFOOT, 1967

After reports of a Bigfoot in Northern California, U.S.A., in 1967, Roger Patterson and Bob Gimlin went into the woods to try to find it. They returned with this famous film footage showing a Bigfoot striding quickly away from the camera.

☐ **FAKE** ☐ **UNEXPLAINED**

5

ANSWERS:

PHOTO 1: FAKE
Edwards later admitted he had faked the photo for fun, using a model hump that he had placed in the water.

PHOTO 2: FAKE (PROBABLY)
Though it hasn't been proven 100 percent yet, close inspection of this photo suggests it is fake. The face on the left has a very hard edge, suggesting it has been cut out and repositioned. The two faces are also incredibly similar, suggesting one could be a copy of the other.

PHOTO 3: FAKE (PROBABLY)
Though people still squabble about the authenticity of this photo, in 2010 a local man might have solved it when he spotted the identical girl in a 1922 postcard of the town. The hair, bonnet, and dress are exactly the same, leading people to think the 1995 photo was most likely doctored.

PHOTO 4: UNEXPLAINED
While some skeptics have claimed the pictures are hoax shots of an object being dangled from a string, many experts think they show a faraway UFO in the sky. They are still debating whether these photos could show a real alien spacecraft.

PHOTO 5: UNEXPLAINED
Many people have pointed out that this "Bigfoot" could be a human in a suit, and some have even come forward to say they were involved in the hoax—but their stories don't match up. The film is still hotly debated, and several experts think it does show a real animal unknown to science. What do you think? Read more about it on page 113.

SHIP OF DOOM

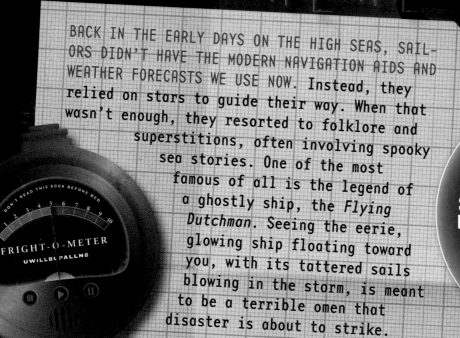

BACK IN THE EARLY DAYS ON THE HIGH SEAS, SAILORS DIDN'T HAVE THE MODERN NAVIGATION AIDS AND WEATHER FORECASTS WE USE NOW. Instead, they relied on stars to guide their way. When that wasn't enough, they resorted to folklore and superstitions, often involving spooky sea stories. One of the most famous of all is the legend of a ghostly ship, the *Flying Dutchman*. Seeing the eerie, glowing ship floating toward you, with its tattered sails blowing in the storm, is meant to be a terrible omen that disaster is about to strike.

THE CAPTAIN IN THE STORY IS SOMETIMES NAMED BERNARD FOKKE, AND SOMETIMES HENDRIK VAN DER DECKEN. BOTH OF THESE WERE REAL CAPTAINS IN THE 1600s—BUT THERE IS NO RECORD OF A REAL *FLYING DUTCHMAN* SHIP.

The legend has been told for hundreds of years. According to the story, in the 1600s, a ship named the *Flying Dutchman* was attempting to sail around the Cape of Good Hope, at the southern tip of Africa. This notoriously stormy spot has been the scene of many shipwrecks. When the weather was too bad, ships often had to shelter in a harbor and wait until the wind died down.

But the captain of the *Flying Dutchman* didn't want to wait. He refused to return to land, swearing that he would get around the Cape if he had to keep sailing until Doomsday (in other words, the end of the world)! Thanks to his stubbornness, the ship promptly sank, along with everyone on board.

Since then, it's said that the tragic ship and her ghostly crew are doomed to sail the ocean forever, never managing to make it around the Cape. According to sailors, seeing her is a warning that someone on board will die, or a ship will be wrecked.

AFRICA

Cape of Good Hope

SPOOKY SHIP SIGHTINGS

Over time, there have been countless reported sightings of the scary ship—especially from the 17th and 18th centuries. The reports vary, but details are similar:

➲ The *Flying Dutchman* appears with tattered sails, often heading toward the shore.

➲ Sometimes she seems to sail faster than any real ship could.

➲ She often hovers in midair, rather than on the sea surface.

➲ She's most likely to appear in stormy weather.

➲ She may shine with an eerie light, sometimes said to be a red glow.

A PAINTING OF THE *FLYING DUTCHMAN*

GHOST LETTERS

According to some stories, the crew of the ghost ship sometimes try to greet sailors, and even send a small boat carrying letters for them to deliver. The letters are addressed to places that don't exist, or people who died long ago. Sailors used to say that the letters should never be taken home, but kept on board ship and nailed to the mast.

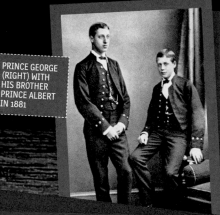

PRINCE GEORGE (RIGHT) WITH HIS BROTHER PRINCE ALBERT IN 1881

ROYAL RUN-IN

In 1881, a British prince, George, who would eventually become King George V, said he had seen the *Dutchman* while he was on board a ship named the H.M.S. *Bacchante*. He wrote in his log:

"At 4 a.m. the *Flying Dutchman* crossed our bows. A strange red light as of a phantom ship all aglow, in the midst of which light the masts, spars and sails ... stood out in strong relief."

He said that 13 crew members had seen the same sight. The first man to spot the *Dutchman* fell from a mast the next day, and died instantly.

MARINE MIRAGE

WHAT COULD BE CAUSING THESE STRANGE GHOST SHIP SIGHTINGS? IS THERE REALLY A GHOST SHIP OUT THERE—OR COULD IT BE SOMETHING ELSE? ONE POSSIBLE EXPLANATION IS A FATA MORGANA, A TYPE OF MIRAGE.

MIRAGES HAPPEN WHEN LIGHT COMING FROM SOMEWHERE IS REFRACTED (OR BENT) AS IT PASSES THROUGH LAYERS OF AIR AT DIFFERENT TEMPERATURES. AT SEA, THIS CAN MAKE LIGHT BEND OVER THE HORIZON. A SHIP THAT IS FAR AWAY AND OUT OF SIGHT CAN SUDDENLY APPEAR, OR SEEM TO BE FLOATING IN THE SKY.

AN EGYPTIAN DESERT MIRAGE

A FATA MORGANA CAN ALSO MAKE ICEBERGS, ISLANDS, AND GIANT WAVES SEEM TO **APPEAR OUT OF NOWHERE**, WHEN THEY ARE NOT REALLY THERE

ZOMBIE FLESH-EATERS

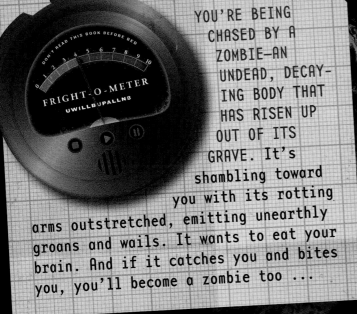

YOU'RE BEING CHASED BY A ZOMBIE—AN UNDEAD, DECAYING BODY THAT HAS RISEN UP OUT OF ITS GRAVE. It's shambling toward you with its rotting arms outstretched, emitting unearthly groans and wails. It wants to eat your brain. And if it catches you and bites you, you'll become a zombie too ...

THE WALKING DEAD

If you've watched a few too many scary movies, you might have a nightmare like this. Weirdly, though, zombies (unlike ghosts) aren't something that many people say they have seen. The Internet isn't full of photos of real-life zombies caught on camera. Yet we all know what a zombie looks like, how it walks, and what it does—partly thanks to all those zombie horror movies, books, and cartoons.

So where did zombies come from, and why are they so frightening?

ZOMBIE WORLD

The idea of zombies is not a new one. In fact, you can find zombielike creatures in folklore, myths, and legends from all around the world.

- In traditional Chinese folklore, there's the *jiangshi*, a pale greenish white dead body that comes hopping after its victims with its arms outstretched, to devour their qi, or life force.

- In Norse legends from Scandinavia, a *draugr* was a zombie-like corpse that rose from the grave and came to eat people, or scare them away from the treasure it guarded. It was blue-black and rotting, incredibly strong, and could increase in size to become a giant zombie.

- In England and Ireland, people told tales of "revenants," the bodies of dead criminals or wrongdoers. They would come back to life to torment people they knew when they were living, or take revenge on their enemies. They sometimes drank blood or ate flesh.

- Even one of the oldest books ever written, the 4,000-year-old *Epic of Gilgamesh*, has a character who says "I will raise up the dead, and they will devour the living"—zombie style!

So it seems dead people coming back to life as terrifying, shambling, flesh-munching ghouls is an age-old fear of humans everywhere!

HISTORY OF THE HORRORS

The zombie tradition familiar in films and cartoons today—and the word "zombie" itself—comes from Haiti, a country in the Caribbean. According to the traditional voodoo beliefs of Haiti, people can be transformed into a half-dead "zombie" state by being given a magical powder. People were said to do this in order to make someone else follow their orders. Over time, this idea combined with others from around the world to create the "undead" flesh-eating zombie.

ZOMBIES ON SCREEN

In the 1930s, stories of zombies from Haiti became popular in the U.S. The film industry had recently taken off, and moviemakers realized zombies would make brilliant movie monsters. Since then, more and more zombie movies, TV shows, books, music videos, and video games have been created. They've become more realistic than ever, so are real-life zombie sightings too far behind?

A PHOTO FROM THE MOVIE *THE PLAGUE OF THE ZOMBIES* FROM 1966

OLD GRAVES HAVE BEEN FOUND IN IRELAND WITH STONES PLACED IN THE MOUTH OF THE BODY. THIS MAY HAVE BEEN DONE TO PREVENT PEOPLE FROM COMING BACK AS REVENANTS.

ZEROING IN ON ZOMBIES

Reports of real zombie sightings are rare, but they have been known to occur in Haiti, where traditional beliefs are still strong. One woman, Felicia Felix-Mentor, was thought to have died in 1907—but reappeared many years later, in 1936, confused, shuffling, and barely aware of her surroundings.

Another "real-life zombie" was Clairvius Narcisse, a Haitian man who apparently died and was buried in 1962. Sixteen years later, he returned to his family, saying he had been dug up from his grave and forced to work as a slave. As this tied in with voodoo customs, everyone believed him.

THE ZOMBIE RULES

The modern idea of a zombie combines several familiar features.

- Zombies groan and mumble, and have a vacant, dumb expression.
- They stagger and limp as they shuffle their decaying bodies around.
- Typically, a zombie holds its arms out straight ahead of it.
- If it bites into you, you will be infected, and will soon turn into a zombie yourself!

COULD IT REALLY HAPPEN?

IS IT POSSIBLE THAT SOMETHING COULD REALLY TURN YOU INTO A ZOMBIE? SOME STUDIES IN HAITI SUGGEST THAT VOODOO PRIESTS DID ONCE HAVE A KIND OF MEDICINE THEY COULD USE TO REDUCE PEOPLE TO A HELPLESS, SHUFFLING ZOMBIFIED STATE, SO THAT THEY COULD CONTROL THEM EASILY. THAT WOULDN'T MAKE THEM REAL, UNDEAD ZOMBIES, THOUGH.

THERE ARE SOME ILLNESSES THAT CAN CHANGE YOUR BEHAVIOR AND MAKE YOU BEHAVE STRANGELY OR VIOLENTLY. ONE IS RABIES, WHICH CAN BE CAUGHT FROM THE BITE OF A BAT OR OTHER WILD ANIMAL, OR SOMETIMES A DOG. RABIES CAN MAKE PEOPLE FEEL CONFUSED, HALLUCINATE, AND FROTH AT THE MOUTH. IT COULD BE THAT PEOPLE WHO WERE SIMPLY SICK GAVE RISE TO THE ZOMBIE LEGEND.

FAIRGROUND FRIGHT!

IN 1976, A FILM CREW PREPARED TO SHOOT A SCENE FOR A TV SHOW AT THE PIKE AMUSEMENT PARK IN LONG BEACH, CALIFORNIA. The scene was set on a ghost ride, and the crew was using a spooky fun house as their set. It was all fun and games until one crew member reached up to move a dangling model of a dead body out of the way. As he did so, the dummy's arm came off—revealing real human bones inside! It wasn't a dummy. It was a mummy!

FRIGHT-O-METER
UWILLBUPALLN8
DON'T READ THIS BOOK BEFORE BED
0 1 2 3 4 5 6 7 8 9 10

The Man Behind THE MUMMY

The police soon arrived and took the body away to be examined and identified. It turned out to be a real, preserved human body, belonging to a train robber who had died 65 years earlier, in 1911. His name was Elmer McCurdy.

Unlike other criminals of his day, McCurdy did not achieve much fame as an outlaw. As a young man, he had spent time in the army and learned to use explosives. Later on he decided to become a robber, and used explosives to blow open a safe full of silver coins on board a train. But he used too much, and the explosion was so big, it melted most of the coins!

Not dissuaded by his first attempt, McCurdy and some friends planned to hold up a train carrying cash. But they targeted a passenger train instead by mistake, and only managed to get away with $46. When the police tracked McCurdy down, he swore they'd never take him alive, and started shooting at the police. He was right—they shot back, and McCurdy was killed.

THE PIKE AMUSEMENT PARK MIDWAY

Claim to FAME

McCurdy's body was sent to a local undertaker. When no relatives came to claim it, the undertaker preserved the body using embalming chemicals, so that it would last until someone wanted it. No one did, so the undertaker put the perfectly preserved corpse on display in his shop as a way of making money. It was labeled "The bandit who wouldn't give up." To see it, visitors had to pay one nickel, and put the nickel in the dead mummy's mouth. Later, the undertaker would collect the coins.

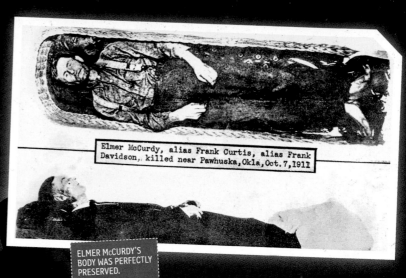

Elmer McCurdy, alias Frank Curtis, alias Frank Davidson, killed near Pawhuska, Okla, Oct. 7, 1911

ELMER McCURDY'S BODY WAS PERFECTLY PRESERVED.

I Want MY MUMMY

One day, several years later, two men came to see the undertaker, claiming that McCurdy was their long-lost brother. It turns out they were actually carnival promoters who wanted a turn at making money off a real dead body. With no proof that they were lying, the undertaker gave up McCurdy, and the mummy spent many years showcased in traveling circuses, museums, and theaters. It was even used as a horror movie prop!

McCurdy was sold and passed on from one owner to the next so many times, people forgot that he was actually a real dead body. By the time he was sold to The Pike amusement park, everyone thought he was just a gruesome (and spookily realistic!) dead body model, made of plastic or wax. So they painted it and hung it up in their fun house.

BURIED at Last

Thanks to a gunshot wound in his chest and money and tickets found in his mouth, investigators were able to figure out who the body belonged to. In 1977, McCurdy's body traveled to Oklahoma, where he had originally died, and was finally given a proper burial.

ENGLISH PHILOSOPHER JEREMY BENTHAM ASKED FOR HIS OWN DEAD BODY TO BE PRESERVED AND PUT ON DISPLAY. HE DIED IN 1832. THE BODY IS NOW IN A GLASS CASE AT A UNIVERSITY IN LONDON.

MEET A MUMMY!

MAKING A MUMMY

NORMALLY, WHEN SOMEONE DIES, THEIR BODY SOON STARTS TO ROT AWAY. UNDERTAKERS CAN STOP THIS FROM HAPPENING BY TREATING THE BODY WITH SUBSTANCES THAT KILL BACTERIA AND PRESERVE THE FLESH. THE UNDERTAKER WHO MUMMIFIED McCURDY USED ARSENIC, A VERY POISONOUS CHEMICAL THAT IS NOW BANNED—BUT FOR MUMMY-MAKING PURPOSES, IT WORKED EXTREMELY WELL! THAT'S WHY HE LASTED SO LONG.

MUMMIES AREN'T ALWAYS INTENTIONALLY MADE. NATURAL MUMMIES HAVE BEEN FOUND IN PEAT BOGS, WHERE THE CHEMICALS IN THE PEAT NATURALLY HAVE THE SAME EFFECT AS CHEMICAL PRESERVATIVES. VERY DRY PLACES ALSO PREVENT DECAY, SO MUMMIES ARE SOMETIMES FOUND IN DESERTS.

A PEAT BOG MUMMY

CREEPS

OF THE DEEP

SCIENTISTS SAY WE KNOW MORE ABOUT SPACE THAN WE DO ABOUT THE OCEANS HERE ON EARTH. WHY IS THAT EXACTLY? Well, about 71 percent of our planet is covered in water, and it's very difficult to get research tools and equipment to the farthest reaches to explore it. After all, in some places the ocean floor is 35,000 feet (10,668 m) below the surface—that's deeper than Mount Everest is tall! What lurks in the black depths of the deepest trenches? The strangest and creepiest creatures you'll ever meet. But luckily for you, you probably never will!

DON'T READ THIS BOOK BEFORE BED

0 1 2 3 4 5 6 7 8 9 10

FRIGHT-O-METER

UWILLBUPALLN8

SLENDER HATCHETFISH

FREAKY FISH

The deep-sea hatchetfish looks like any other fish in the ocean ... that came back to life as a zombie to haunt the deep! But this freaky-featured fish is no fiend, and there are reasons for its weird appearance. Its enormous round eyeballs are good at collecting the tiniest amounts of light. Sunlight doesn't reach the bottom of the deep sea, so it's very dark down there. The hatchetfish's eyes scan the water above to try to detect any sign of tasty prey swimming above it. Then it uses its gaping mouth to snap up its meal.

Don't be too scared, though—it may look monstrous, but the hatchetfish is actually really small, and could fit in your hand!

SLIME TIME!

Want to see a magic trick? Drop a hagfish into a bucket of water, and the water will all turn into revolting, stringy slime in minutes! Hagfish release slime-making chemicals to make it harder for other sea creatures to grab and eat them. But what's more menacing is how these deep-sea horrors go about eating their own lunch—which involves using their faceful of sharp teeth to burrow right inside another animal's dead body and munch it from the inside out! Talk about a nightmare!

HAGFISH

HELPFUL HAGFISH

HAGFISH SLIME MAY BE DISGUSTING, BUT IT COULD ALSO BE INCREDIBLY USEFUL. SCIENTISTS HAVE STUDIED THE SLIME AND FOUND THAT IT CONTAINS THOUSANDS OF VERY THIN, STRETCHY STING-LIKE STRANDS. THEY HOLD THE SLIME TOGETHER AND MAKE IT STRINGY AND ELASTIC. THE SLIME STRINGS CAN BE COLLECTED AND DRIED OUT, AND COULD BE USED TO MAKE A TYPE OF SUPERSTRONG, STRETCHY FABRIC, FOR MAKING SPORTSWEAR OR PROTECTIVE GEAR, FOR EXAMPLE. OR, IF WE CAN FIGURE OUT HOW THE STRINGS ARE MADE, WE COULD COPY THEM AND USE THEM TO INSPIRE A NEW, HI-TECH SYNTHETIC FABRIC.

HAGFISH HAVE FOUR HEARTS, BUT NO SKELETON, APART FROM THEIR SKULL.

BEWARE OF THE BLOB!

Hovering just above the deep seafloor, on the lookout for food drifting past, is the spectacularly strange-looking, pink, rubbery blobfish. Blob by name, and blob by nature, this fish is not great at swimming, or even moving much! It has very little muscle, as it's mostly made up of a jellylike substance that allows it to bob gently around instead of sinking. We rarely see blobfish, except when they are accidentally caught in fishing nets and pulled to the surface.

In most photos you'll see of a blobfish that has been caught, it has an amazingly floppy, mournful-looking face. It doesn't look quite so weird when it's at home in the deep ocean, though, as the water holds its body up. And if you do happen across one on your line, rest assured, they're about as ferocious as they appear.

BLOBFISH

SPOOKY SHARK

Fast, sleek, sharp-toothed hunting machines—pretty much describes all sharks, right? Well, maybe some of them. But not this freakish fellow!

For a start, the goblin shark is pinkish gray in color, and has a strangely soft, flabby body. Its snout is flat, like a pointed shovel blade. The goblin shark can't swim fast, but instead waits for prey—such as an octopus—to come close, and then suddenly strikes and grabs it, similar to the way a snake hunts. To help it seize its food, it can thrust its jaws right out from under its snout, like a pair of toothy tongs. Super scary, yes, but there's good news: Goblin sharks have never been known to eat humans.

GOBLIN SHARK

THE BEAST OF BODMIN

FRIGHT-O-METER
DON'T READ THIS BOOK BEFORE BED
0 1 2 3 4 5 6 7 8 9 10
UWILLBUPALLN8

BODMIN MOOR IS A SERIOUSLY SPOOKY PLACE. This stretch of bleak, misty moorland in Cornwall, England, is believed to be haunted by several ghosts, including Charlotte Dymond, who was killed there in 1844. The moor also has links to legendary King Arthur, who was said to have died at the supposedly bottomless Dozmary Pool. It's not a place you want to visit on a dark night! But ghosts and peculiar puddles are just the beginning of your worries ...

IN 2012, POLICE IN EDINBURGH, SCOTLAND, WERE SEARCHING A HILLSIDE BY HELICOPTER WHEN THEY SPOTTED A HUGE, COUGAR-LIKE BIG CAT IN THE BUSHES.

I SPY ...

One of the moor's creepiest residents is not supernatural, but instead, a mysterious, ferocious big cat called the Beast of Bodmin Moor. Dozens of people have reported seeing it. There are several photos and even videos of the Beast. For decades, farmers have described a big cat that has stalked and eaten their sheep and lambs. Yet there's still no absolute proof. So what is it? And more important, is it a danger to humans?

THE EURASIAN LYNX

BRITISH BIG CATS

Big cats, such as tigers, lions, and jaguars, are not native to Britain. British wildlife has not included any big cats since medieval times, when the Eurasian lynx lived there. The Beast of Bodmin, though, is nothing like a lynx. Lynxes aren't very big, and they're usually a golden color.

The Beast, on the other hand, is usually described as large and black or brown. It has several other distinctive features too ...

COULD THE BEAST BE A JAGUAR?

MEET THE BEAST

- ➲ Large—usually described as well over three feet (1 m) long
- ➲ Long, furry tail
- ➲ Smallish head, like that of a cougar
- ➲ Yellow or whitish yellow eyes

Locals say the Beast can also be heard at night. Its sounds include:
- ➲ Growling
- ➲ Hissing
- ➲ A loud shriek, like a person screaming

Farmers also claim they can tell when the Beast has killed their sheep. Unlike a dog or fox, it kills the animal cleanly with its strong jaws and claws, and eats the meat, leaving no mess. Well, cats are known to be very clean and fastidious—even big cats!

SPOT THE DIFFERENCE

BIG CATS LIKE COUGARS AND JAGUARS ARE CLOSELY RELATED TO PET CATS. BUT THEY DO HAVE SOME KEY DIFFERENCES THAT YOU CAN USE TO HELP YOU SPOT WHICH IS WHICH.

BLACK CAT
- ➲ Fluffy coat
- ➲ Large head and ears compared to body size
- ➲ Fluffy, wide tail
- ➲ Delicate paws

BLACK PANTHER (A BLACK LEOPARD OR JAGUAR)
- ➲ Stronger neck and shoulder muscles
- ➲ Smoother coat
- ➲ Smaller head and ears compared to body size
- ➲ Longer, narrow tail
- ➲ Bigger paws
- ➲ Bigger teeth

YOU CAN EVEN CREATE YOUR OWN BEAST OF BODMIN MOOR WITH YOUR PET CAT (IF YOUR CAT WILL COOPERATE!). TAKE THE PHOTO FROM A LOW ANGLE, CLOSE TO THE GROUND. HAVE A FRIEND OR FAMILY MEMBER STAND A LONG WAY BEHIND THE CAT, SO THAT THEY LOOK SMALL—MAKING THE CAT APPEAR LARGER. YOU HAVE YOUR VERY OWN BEAST.

SOLVING THE MYSTERY

There are several theories that could explain the Beast of Bodmin Moor.

➲ IT'S AN ESCAPED ZOO ANIMAL
It's possible that a big cat, such as a panther or cougar, could escape from a zoo, or from a private, illegal animal collection. However, to keep being spotted for as long as it has, there would have to be a population of several animals on the moor to supply new generations of the beast.

➲ IT'S SOMETHING PARANORMAL AND SPOOKY
Given the moor's haunted reputation, some people think the Bodmin Beast must be some kind of giant ghost cat. But a ghost that can eat an animal down to the bones? Now that's a chilling thought!

➲ IT'S JUST A BIG KITTY CAT!
Some of the photos taken of the "Beast of Bodmin" are probably just normal black pet cats. In some photos of cats, it can be hard to tell how big they are.

➲ IT'S SOMETHING ELSE
Other suggestions for animals the Beast could be include a fox, a wild boar, a deer, or a dog that looks a bit like a cat.

➲ IT'S A HOAX
As with other unexplained and spooky mysteries, some of the photos could have been faked.

TONGUE TAKEOVER!

FRIGHT-O-METER

0 1 2 3 4 5 6 7 8 9 10

UWIL BUPALLN8

THE THOUGHT OF CREEPY-CRAWLIES MIGHT SEND SHIVERS DOWN YOUR SPINE, BUT IMAGINE ONE GETTING IN YOUR MOUTH! Now imagine it eating your tongue. Now picture the menacing little monster taking its place and living as your tongue! Sounds like a disgusting, stomach-churning, wake-up-in-a-cold-sweat nightmare, right? Well here's the bad part: There is a real-life creature that does this—and it's called, unsurprisingly, the tongue-eating louse.

MENACING METHOD

BEFORE YOU SCREAM IN TERROR AND MAKE SURE YOUR TONGUE IS INTACT, THERE'S GOOD NEWS: This louse much prefers fish tongues over our own. You might be wondering, how can something possibly eat your tongue and live in its place? Here's how this tiny terror accomplishes its task:

When it's a baby, the teeny little louse wriggles in through a fish's gills, and makes its way toward the tongue. (Did you even know fish have tongues? Some do, although they don't move them around as much as humans do.) The louse doesn't target all types of fish—just a few, such as the rose snapper.

Once it's there, the tongue-eating louse grips onto the base of the fish's tongue with its claws, and begins to suck blood out of the tongue. This makes the tongue wither up, die, and drop off. After that, the louse just stays there, where the tongue used to be. It sucks the fish's blood or feeds on the mucus in its mouth. The fish doesn't die—it can keep on living and feeding, using the tongue louse instead of a tongue.

SHOPPING

NOW YOU MAY THINK YOU'RE IN THE CLEAR FOR AVOIDING THESE UNWANTED INVADERS, BUT HERE'S WHERE IT CAN AFFECT YOU: As they live in fishes' mouths, tongue lice sometimes end up being caught in a fishing net along with their fish hosts. In other words, they can end up on your dinner plate. Unsuspecting shoppers were in for quite a scare when they found a creepy tongue louse inside a fish they had bought from the market, and cooked up for dinner. (Though experts say you could eat a tongue louse without it doing you any harm. It would probably taste kind of like a shrimp.)

PIKE PLACE FISH MARKET, SEATTLE, WASHINGTON, U.S.A.

FREAKY FAMILY

IF THE TONGUE LOUSE LOOKS A LITTLE FAMILIAR, THAT COULD BE BECAUSE IT'S RELATED TO SEVERAL OTHER BETTER-KNOWN ANIMALS. It's a crustacean, like crabs, prawns, and lobsters. It's even more closely related to pill bugs, which live on land, and the terrifying-looking giant isopod, a sea creature that looks like a ginormous, white, alien robot pillbug. This huge deep-sea creature feeds on dead, rotting animals and slow-moving creatures, such as sea slugs.

GIANT ISOPOD

A SADDLEBACK ANEMONEFISH WITH A TONGUE-EATING LOUSE IN ITS MOUTH

LADY LICE

ANOTHER STRANGE THING ABOUT TONGUE LICE IS THAT THEY CAN CHANGE FROM MALE TO FEMALE. They are born male, but if two lice end up in the same fish, one will turn into a girl. She's the one that latches onto the fish's tongue. The female will then have her babies in the fish's mouth! The babies swim away to find new fish to live in.

PETRIFYING PARASITES

THOUGH THE TONGUE LOUSE IS CALLED A LOUSE, IT'S ACTUALLY A CRUSTACEAN AND NOT A TRUE LOUSE. REAL LICE ARE A TYPE OF INSECT. THEY ARE ALSO PARASITES—CREATURES THAT LIVE ON AND GET THEIR FOOD FROM ANOTHER LIVING THING. THE CREATURE THEY LIVE ON IS KNOWN AS THE HOST.

THOUGH YOU DON'T HAVE TO WORRY ABOUT YOUR TONGUE BEING EATEN, THERE ARE PLENTY OF GROSS PARASITES THAT DO LIVE ON HUMAN BEINGS.

→ THE **HUMAN LOUSE** LIVES ON PEOPLE'S SKIN AND INSIDE CLOTHES, AND BITES ITS HOST TO SUCK THEIR BLOOD. THESE LICE ARE LESS COMMON THAN THEY USED TO BE IN THE DAYS WHEN PEOPLE DIDN'T BATHE OR WASH THEIR CLOTHES QUITE AS MUCH.

→ **HEAD LICE** LIVE ON PEOPLE'S HEADS, CLING TO THEIR HAIR, AND BITE THEIR SCALPS. THEY LAY TINY WHITE LEGS, WHICH ARE KNOWN AS NITS.

→ **EYELASH MITES** LIVE IN AND AROUND PEOPLE'S EYELASHES. THEY NIBBLE ON DEAD SKIN CELLS, AND ON THE SEBUM, OR OIL, THAT IS RELEASED FROM THE SKIN. MOST PEOPLE HAVE THESE MITES, BUT THEY ARE TEENY, HARMLESS, AND YOU NEVER NOTICE THEM.

AN EYELASH MITE, MAGNIFIED

ISLAND OF THE DOLLS

FRIGHT-O-METER
UWILLBUPAL_N8
0 1 2 3 4 5 6 7 8 9 10
DON'T READ THIS BOOK BEFORE BED

IN MEXICO CITY, AMONG A NETWORK OF OLD CANALS, STAND SMALL, ARTIFICIAL ISLANDS, OR CHINAMPAS, BUILT BY THE AZTECS HUNDREDS OF YEARS AGO. Some are used as farms or gardens, but one island stands out among the rest. Why? It's covered with trees and bushes, like the others, but dangling from their branches are more than a thousand dirty, broken baby dolls, all staring at you with their wide-open eyes.

This spine-tinglingly spooky place is called La Isla de las Muñecas, or the Island of the Dolls. These days, it's a destination for tourists to visit on a canal boat day trip. In the past, though, it was the home of a reclusive local man, Julian Santana Barrera, who created the creepy doll display over many years.

Ghost of a **GIRL**

According to local legend, Barrera moved to the island in 1950. Around that time, he claimed that a young girl had drowned in the canal near his island—though there's no record that this actually happened. No one knows if it's true, or was something Barrera imagined or made up.

Whatever really happened, Barrera began to believe the island, where he lived in a small hut, was being haunted by the girl's ghost. When he found a doll floating in the canal, he decided it must belong to her. He fished it out and hung it up on a tree, to try to keep the girl's spirit happy.

But for some reason, Barrera felt this wasn't enough. He began adding more and more old, abandoned dolls, which he found among trash floating in the canals, or dug out of dumpsters. Friends also brought him dolls in exchange for the fruit and vegetables he grew in his garden. Hanging up on the trees, they became more and more weathered and worn, covered in moss and mold, and broken, making a creepy display even more unsettling.

After Barrera died in 2001, his nephew took over the island, and made it into a tourist attraction. It's become well-known around the world and has been featured in magazines and TV shows.

A MOSS-COVERED DOLL HANGS FROM A TREE.

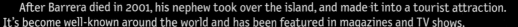

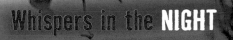

ISLAND OF THE DOLLS

Whispers in the NIGHT

Local people still believe the island is haunted. They claim the dolls are possessed by spirits, and that at night, they come alive—slowly, creakily moving their limbs, turning their heads, and whispering to each other. Understandably, most people just come for a quick look around, rather than stick around overnight. Perhaps it's for the best, as since his death, Barrera himself is also said to haunt the island.

Seeing THINGS

The island is definitely eerie, but is it really haunted by a young girl's ghost? Some people think it's more likely that Barrera imagined or hallucinated the things he spoke about. Late in his life, he also claimed that there were mermaids living in the canals, who he liked to talk to and play music to. But no one else ever saw them! This suggests he often saw things that weren't really there, and that the "haunting" was not real.

THE ISLA DE LAS MUÑECAS (ISLAND OF THE DOLLS) IS ACTUALLY A FLOATING GARDEN.

MOANING CAVERN

SPOOKY SPOTS

WANT SOME OTHER SCARY PLACES TO VISIT? TRY THESE ...

- MOANING CAVERN IN CALIFORNIA, U.S.A., IS A HUGE, DEEP CAVE THAT MAKES A MYSTERIOUS MOANING SOUND (ACTUALLY CAUSED BY DRIPPING WATER, AIR CURRENTS, AND ECHOES). ANCIENT SKELETONS HAVE ALSO BEEN FOUND INSIDE IT.

- CLOUTIE WELLS, FOUND IN PARTS OF THE U.K., ARE WELLS THAT WERE ONCE BELIEVED TO HAVE MAGICAL HEALING POWERS. TO BE CURED, A SICK PERSON WOULD TAKE A CLOTH, DIP IT INTO THE WATER, AND TIE IT TO A NEARBY TREE—RESULTING IN EERIE TREES COVERED WITH THOUSANDS OF RAGGED CLOTHS.

- ENGLAND'S ROLLRIGHT STONES ARE SAID TO BE A KING AND HIS MEN WHO WERE TURNED INTO A CIRCLE OF STONES BY A WITCH. ACCORDING TO LEGEND, THEY SOMETIMES COME BACK TO LIFE AT MIDNIGHT. IT'S SAID THAT YOU CAN'T COUNT THE STONES—WHENEVER YOU TRY, YOU'LL ALWAYS GET A DIFFERENT NUMBER.

NOT WHO I USED TO BE

DO YOU BELIEVE THAT YOU HAD A PAST LIFE, BEFORE YOU BEGAN THIS ONE? Many cultures around the world believe in reincarnation—that when we die, our soul is born in a new body. Of the many people who believe it's possible, some even say they can remember their past lives! Oftentimes, it's small children who describe details of a different life before they were born—much to the amazement of their parents! But is it real, or could it just be kids recounting details of something they read, heard, or saw on TV? Whatever you think, these stories may convince you.

FRIGHT-O-METER

DON'T READ THIS BOOK BEFORE BED
0 1 2 3 4 5 6 7 8 9 10
UWILLBU ALLN8

I WAS A PILOT!

James Leininger, from Lafayette, Louisiana, U.S.A., was obsessed with airplanes pretty much since he was born. But around age two, he began to have nightmares. He would wake up shouting that he was inside a burning plane and couldn't escape.

His parents didn't think much of it, until it happened repeatedly, and James gave more and more details about the crash scenario. He said that he was a pilot, also named James, and his plane had been shot down by the Japanese. He had taken off from a ship named *Natoma*, and he had a friend named Jack Larsen. He also could name different plane parts, how they worked, and what they were used for—despite never having been taught.

His baffled parents did some research and discovered his story matched the details of a real-life pilot named James Huston who died in 1945 at the Battle of Iwo Jima during World War II. He had, in fact, flown from the aircraft carrier *Natoma*, and he had a friend named Jack Larsen. He also flew a Corsair aircraft, which is the exact type of plane that James Leininger had described!

JAMES LEININGER AT AGE TWO

SHANTI DEVI

On December 11, 1926, a baby girl named Shanti Devi was born in Delhi, India. At age four, she began to tell her parents about her old family—and wanted to look for them. She said they lived in Mathura, a town about 100 miles (161 km) away, and ran a cloth shop. She also said she had a husband and a son. She remembered the things she used to wear and eat during her life in Mathura, and described her husband in detail, including his glasses. She also explained that she had died after having her baby son.

She was so insistent that eventually her family and teachers decided to see if it was true. They managed to find a cloth seller living in Mathura with the name Shanti had given, Kedarnath Chaube. They contacted him and his son and arranged for them to visit Shanti.

Shanti recognized her "husband" at once, knew his favorite foods, and gave lots of accurate details about his house. His wife, Lugdi, had died nine days after giving birth to their son, in 1925—just over a year before Shanti's birth.

THE MONASTERY IN PETRA, JORDAN

ARTHUR FLOWERDEW

Usually, children speak about their past-life memories as soon as they can talk, and stop mentioning them by the age of five or six. But Arthur Flowerdew was different. Growing up in Norfolk, England, he had repeated visions and memories of a pink stone city, with a temple carved into a cliff. The older he got, the more he "remembered" about the city, though he had no idea what it was. Then, as an adult, he saw a television show about the ancient city of Petra in Jordan, and recognized it as "his" city.

After Arthur himself was featured in a TV show about past-life memories, the government of Jordan arranged for him to visit Petra. Once there, he discovered that he could easily find his way around, though he had supposedly never been there (in this lifetime)! He explained to archaeologists what various buildings were for, and pointed out locations of things that had not yet been excavated. The archaeologists were amazed by the details he knew.

PAUL GAUGUIN

WHEN PEOPLE SAY THEY HAD A PAST LIFE, IT OFTEN SEEMS TO HAVE BEEN AS A FAMOUS PERSON! FAMOUS FIGURES HAVE INCLUDED THE ARTIST PAUL GAUGUIN, ABRAHAM LINCOLN, AND THE HOLLYWOOD MOVIE STAR JEAN HARLOW.

WHY DOES IT HAPPEN?

SO WHY DO SOME PEOPLE BELIEVE THEY REMEMBER A PAST LIFE? EXPERTS ARE SKEPTICAL, BUT PEOPLE WHO BELIEVE THEY HAVE EXPERIENCED REINCARNATION SEEM TO HAVE ONE THING IN COMMON: THEY ALL SAY THEY DIED IN A SUDDEN OR VIOLENT WAY. COULD IT BE THAT THEY DIDN'T FINISH LIVING THEIR LIFE, SO THEY HAD TO COME BACK AND START A NEW ONE?

IN INVESTIGATIONS, IT'S OFTEN HARD TO PROVE THAT THE PERSON COULD NOT HAVE KNOWN ABOUT THE DETAILS OF THEIR "PREVIOUS" LIFE ANOTHER WAY. FOR EXAMPLE, ARTHUR FLOWERDEW CLAIMED HE HAD NEVER HEARD OF PETRA, BUT HE COULD HAVE READ ABOUT IT AS A CHILD. HOWEVER, QUITE A FEW EXAMPLES ARE REALLY CREEPY, AND CAN'T EASILY BE EXPLAINED. IS IT JUST SOMETHING STRANGE THAT SOME CHILDREN DO ... OR IS IT EVIDENCE OF LIFE AFTER DEATH? THE IDEA THAT PEOPLE CAN LIVE OVER AND OVER AGAIN IS CERTAINLY COMFORTING TO SOME.

ABANDONED SHIP!

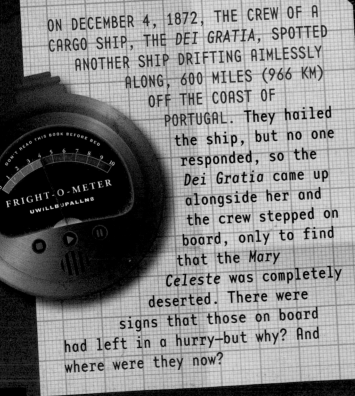

ON DECEMBER 4, 1872, THE CREW OF A CARGO SHIP, THE *DEI GRATIA*, SPOTTED ANOTHER SHIP DRIFTING AIMLESSLY ALONG, 600 MILES (966 KM) OFF THE COAST OF PORTUGAL. They hailed the ship, but no one responded, so the *Dei Gratia* came up alongside her and the crew stepped on board, only to find that the Mary Celeste was completely deserted. There were signs that those on board had left in a hurry—but why? And where were they now?

DON'T READ THIS BOOK BEFORE BED
0 1 2 3 4 5 6 7 8 9 10
FRIGHT-O-METER
UWILLBUPALLN8

The *Mary Celeste* had set sail almost a month earlier, setting off across the Atlantic Ocean from New York, bound for Genoa, Italy. She was carrying a cargo of 1,700 barrels of a chemical called ethanol, which catches fire easily. On board were the experienced captain, Benjamin Briggs; his wife, Sarah; their two-year-old daughter, Sophia; and seven crewmen. All of them had vanished.

The ship was in good working order, although one of the pumps used for pumping seawater out of the hold was broken, and some of the cargo barrels had leaked. The people on board had left behind their food and water supplies, and their personal belongings and valuables. Oilskin waterproofs, navigation charts, and the crewmen's pipes had all been left lying around.

However, they had taken the chronometer and sextant—equipment for calculating where you are at sea—and one lifeboat. And trailing in the sea behind the ship, the men of the *Dei Gratia* found a single, loose rope ...

SEA STORIES

The 10 missing people were never found, and their strange disappearance became a famous mystery. Sensationalist accounts of the tragedy appeared in newspapers. Author Sir Arthur Conan Doyle, who later created the detective Sherlock Holmes, wrote a short story about the disaster, making it even more famous. Around the world, people came up with all kinds of theories about what might have happened—but most of them didn't seem to hold water.

- ➲ A giant squid or sea monster had devoured the sailors (and their lifeboat and navigation tools!).

- ➲ Pirates from nearby Morocco had raided the ship. (Except they had left the valuable cargo untouched.)

- ➲ A deadly waterspout had whirled them all off the deck.

- ➲ The crew had turned against the captain and killed him and his family, before fleeing in the lifeboat. (Unlikely, as there had been no previous problems.)

- ➲ Fumes from substances inside the barrels on board had caused a huge explosion, so everyone abandoned ship. However, there was no soot, charring, or sign of fire.

IS THIS WHAT MIGHT HAVE HAPPENED TO THE CREW OF THE *MARY CELESTE*?

WHAT REALLY HAPPENED?

TO THIS DAY, NO ONE KNOWS FOR CERTAIN WHY THE *MARY CELESTE* WAS ABANDONED, OR WHERE EVERYONE WENT. HOWEVER, EXPERTS DO HAVE A FAVORITE THEORY:

FOR A LONG TIME, THE IDEA OF AN EXPLOSION WAS DISMISSED, AS THERE WAS NO SIGN OF FIRE DAMAGE. BUT IN 2006, A SCIENTIST DID AN EXPLOSIVE EXPERIMENT TO SEE IF IT COULD ACTUALLY BE TRUE. HE MADE A MODEL OF THE SHIP, AND FILLED IT WITH PAPER CUBES TO REPRESENT THE BARRELS. THEN HE SET FIRE TO SOME BUTANE GAS, CAUSING A GAS EXPLOSION IN THE MODEL'S HOLD. THERE WAS A BIG BANG AND FLAMES, BUT THE PAPER WASN'T SCORCHED OR DAMAGED AT ALL. ONLY THE GAS CAUGHT FIRE.

THIS SUGGESTS THERE COULD HAVE BEEN A BIG EXPLOSION ON BOARD THE SHIP, CAUSED BY FUMES FROM THE BARRELS OF ETHANOL. IN A PANIC, THE CAPTAIN ORDERED EVERYONE INTO THE LIFEBOAT, AND TIED IT BEHIND THE SHIP, PLANNING TO RETURN ONCE THE FLAMES DIED DOWN. BUT THE ROPE CAME LOOSE, AND THE LIFEBOAT WAS LOST AT SEA.

THE BAD-LUCK SHIP

Some people have pointed out that a lot of unlucky things happened to the *Mary Celeste*. Originally called the *Amazon*, its name had only been changed to the *Mary Celeste* after a string of disasters:

- ➲ The ship's first captain had died of pneumonia after just nine days on board.

- ➲ Later on her maiden voyage, the ship crashed and had to be repaired.

- ➲ While she was being repaired, a fire broke out!

- ➲ On her first trip across the Atlantic Ocean, the *Amazon* hit another ship.

- ➲ After that, she ran aground.

Perhaps the *Mary Celeste* was jinxed! Or could there be a more sensible explanation?

OR COULD IT HAVE BEEN A SEA MONSTER?

THE WOW! SIGNAL

FRIGHT-O-METER

DON'T READ THIS BOOK BEFORE BED

UWIL_BUPALLN8

DO YOU THINK ALIENS EXIST, SOMEWHERE OUT THERE ON ANOTHER WORLD? Or are we all alone, the only planet in the whole universe that is home to living things? Of course, it's very hard to be sure—but if there are other intelligent, advanced life-forms out there, you would think that they might have tried to send us a message by now. Well, maybe they have!

THE SEARCH FOR E.T.

THE ALMA TELESCOPES—ONE OF THE MOST POWERFUL TELESCOPE ARRAYS IN THE WORLD

FOR CENTURIES, HUMANS HAVE WONDERED ABOUT THE POSSIBILITY OF LIFE ON OTHER PLANETS. Around 1900, we first discovered radio waves and how they could be used to send signals over long distances. Scientists realized that they would be a good way to make contact with intelligent life-forms on other planets, or for them to make contact with us.

From then on, astrobiologists began to look out for messages or information in the form of radio signals from space. This became known as SETI—the Search for Extraterrestrial Intelligence.

One way to look out for alien messages is using huge, powerful radio telescopes to scan the sky. One of the first telescopes to do this was called the Big Ear. It was built at Ohio State University in the 1960s. Volunteers would check the results from the telescope, looking out for anything unusual.

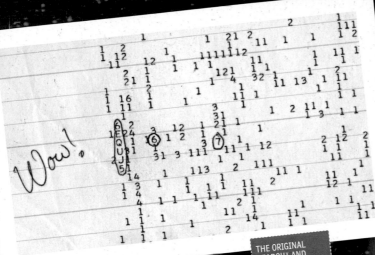

WOW!

IN 1977, A BIG EAR VOLUNTEER NAMED JERRY EHMAN WAS LOOKING THROUGH PAGES OF RESULTS. AS USUAL, THEY WERE PRETTY TYPICAL FOR RADIO SILENCE—AND REVEALED NOTHING, EXCEPT THE NORMAL LOW LEVEL OF RADIO WAVES THAT BOUNCE AROUND IN SPACE. The telescope's readout showed these as low numbers such as 1, 2, and 3, or empty spaces, which stood for zero.

Then, in among the background numbers, Ehman suddenly spotted an incredibly unusual set of figures. They were much, much higher than the rest, and also formed a particular pattern—a signal that increased from faint to very strong, then faded out again. It was unlike anything the telescope had picked up before, and unlike any known natural radio waves from space. Ehman picked up his red pen, circled the signal and wrote "Wow!"

UNDERSTANDING
THE SIGNAL

TO NONSCIENTISTS, THIS BUNCH OF NUMBERS AND LETTERS MIGHT NOT LOOK ALL THAT REMARKABLE. To understand what it means, you have to know a few things about how the readout worked. When the telescope picked up radio activity, it gave it a rating depending on how strong it was. The ratings ran from 0 to 9, and then, because each rating had to be a single figure, they switched to the letters of the alphabet. So the scale looked like this:

0 1 2 3 4 5 6 7 8 9 A B C D E F G H I J K L M N O P Q R S T U V W X Y Z

The Wow! signal read: **6 E Q U J 5**—a series of very high numbers in a background of mainly 0s, 1s, and 2s. If you showed it as a spike on a graph, it would look something like this:

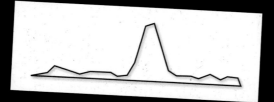

It was a superstrong stand-alone signal. However, when scientists scanned the same area of sky to see if the signal would be repeated, they found nothing.

ANYBODY OUT
THERE?

NOT CONTENT WITH JUST LISTENING FOR SIGNALS, HUMANS HAVE ALSO BEEN SENDING OUT OUR OWN MESSAGES INTO SPACE FOR ANYONE WHO MIGHT BE LISTENING.

IN 1974, A RADIO BROADCAST WAS BEAMED OUT INTO SPACE FROM ARECIBO, PUERTO RICO. IT CONTAINED A SIMPLE DIGITAL IMAGE SHOWING PICTURES OF NUMBERS, CHEMICALS, THE SOLAR SYSTEM, AND A HUMAN.

IN 1977, TWO SPACE PROBES, VOYAGER 1 AND 2, SET OUT FROM EARTH ON A LONG-DISTANCE MISSION INTO OUTER SPACE. (THEY'RE STILL GOING!) EACH HAS A "GOLDEN RECORD" ON BOARD, CONTAINING SOUNDS, PICTURES, AND GREETINGS FROM EARTH.

IN 2012, A REPLY TO THE WOW! SIGNAL, MADE UP OF TWITTER MESSAGES, WAS ALSO SENT FROM ARECIBO. IT WAS AIMED AT THE AREA OF SPACE THE SIGNAL HAD COME FROM.

MYSTERY
SOLVED?

THE WOW! SIGNAL REMAINS THE MOST CONVINCING EVIDENCE YET THAT SOMEONE OR SOMETHING IN SPACE COULD BE SENDING OUT MESSAGES DELIBERATELY. However, in 2016, one scientist claimed he had solved the mystery, saying the signal could have been made by energy from a faraway comet. However, this hasn't been proven.

MONSTER JELLIES

RIGHT NOW, AT THIS VERY MOMENT, THERE'S SOMETHING LURKING IN THE WATERY VASTNESS OF THE OCEANS THAT WOULD CERTAINLY MAKE YOU THINK TWICE ABOUT TAKING A TRIP TO THE BEACH EVER AGAIN. It's huge, menacing, and packs a punch so powerful it's sometimes deadly. No, we're not talking about great whites—but a brainless blob that is even more common. Read on to discover why jellies are the real monsters of the deep—and which ones you need to definitely steer clear of.

DON'T READ THIS BOOK BEFORE BED

0 1 2 3 4 5 6 7 8 9 10

FRIGHT-O-METER
UWILLBUPALLN8

NOMURA'S JELLY-FISH OFF THE COAST OF JAPAN

JELLYFISH DON'T HAVE BRAINS! BUT SOME DO HAVE EYES, AND CAN MOVE TOWARD AND CHASE THEIR PREY.

THE BIGGEST JELLYFISH

Just how big can a jellyfish grow? It all depends on the species, but the lion's mane jellyfish is probably the most monstrous of all. The biggest ever found measured more than seven feet (2 m) across the bell, or upper part, with tentacles stretching more than 120 feet (36 m) long. That means the bell was bigger than a double bed, and the tentacles were as long as three school buses! And just to make things weirder, this giant jelly can also glow in the dark.

So does that mean a giant jellyfish could actually swallow up a human? It certainly looks as if it could ... but it's not actually possible. A diver could maybe get tangled up in the tentacles, but there are no reports of anyone being eaten alive. That's because even big jellyfish have quite small mouths, so a human would be too big to swallow. Instead, they feed on much smaller prey, such as tiny fish or plankton.

A DIVER AND A GIANT PELAGIC JELLYFISH

TINY TERRORS

But that doesn't mean jellyfish aren't dangerous. Many species have stinging tentacles that inject a painful venom into anything they touch. Some just hurt a lot, while others are lethal. Box jellyfish are much smaller than the lion's mane, but their powerful venom can kill a person in just a few minutes. In fact, the box jelly's venom is thought to be the deadliest of any animal in the world!

What's even more spine-tingling is that the deadliest of all box jellyfish is the Irukandji, which measures only half an inch (1 cm) across! It's also transparent, so if you can see it coming at all, you might mistake it for a speck of shrimp or even plankton.

AN IRUKANDJI SPECIMEN

JELLYFISH ARE NOT ACTUALLY FISH. THEY ARE A TYPE OF INVERTEBRATE, AND DON'T HAVE BONES. IN FACT, A JELLYFISH IS ABOUT 98 PERCENT WATER.

BLOOM OF DOOM

Think one of these jellies is creepy? Well, what about a swarm of millions of them?! A big group of jellyfish is called a bloom, and they can cause major problems—in addition to terrifying swimmers who happen across one. If jellyfish have plenty of food (like fish, fish eggs, shrimp, sea slugs, or even smaller jellyfish) they can multiply fast. Suddenly, a ginormous bloom can grow to fill a huge area of water. Jelly blooms have destroyed fish farms by killing all the fish, and forced power stations to switch off by clogging up their water pipes. They can fill up harbors and make it impossible to go fishing or swimming.

What's even worse—scientists think there are more jellyfish blooms than ever before. While climate change and ocean pollution are bad for most wildlife, they seem to create perfect breeding grounds for more jellyfish! Some experts say jellies could eventually take over the seas, replacing most other life-forms in the oceans.

JUMPIN' JELLYFISH

DON'T BELIEVE EVERYTHING YOU SEE ... THIS IMAGE OF A GIANT JELLYFISH ALONGSIDE A DIVER IS REAL, BUT SOME IMAGES OF THE NOMURA JELLY CAN BE DECEIVING. THE IMAGE, WHICH HAS BEEN CIRCULATING ON THE INTERNET FOR YEARS, IS NOT ENTIRELY WHAT IT SEEMS. IT SHOWS A DIVER FARTHER AWAY FROM THE CAMERA THAN THE JELLY, MAKING THE MONSTER APPEAR 10 TIMES ITS REAL SIZE! PHOTOS LIKE THESE OFTEN GO VIRAL AND ARE SHARED HUNDREDS OF THOUSANDS, EVEN MILLIONS, OF TIMES. BUT THERE AREN'T ACTUALLY ANY JELLYFISH THE SIZE OF A HOUSE. (WELL, THERE COULD BE ... MAYBE WE JUST HAVEN'T DISCOVERED THEM YET!)

A JELLYFISH BLOOM

QUIZ

HOW WOOOOOOOO ARE YOU?

HOW SCARED YOU'LL BE BY THE THINGS IN THIS BOOK DEPENDS ON YOUR BELIEFS AND OUTLOOK. Are you an eyebrow-raising skeptic who has some serious doubts about ghosts, telepathy, and other mysterious mumbo jumbo? Or are you a true believer in supernatural, magical events that can't be explained by science? This kind of paranormal and unexplained stuff is sometimes known as "woo."

So ... just how woo are you?

ONCE WOO, NOW TRUE!

I'M A BELIEVER!

Boo! It's OK, it's not really a ghost! But it's fair to say you're pretty spooked out by all kinds of strange, creepy, and spine-tingling things. Ghosts, cryptids, psychic predictions—you're sure there's more to this world than meets the eye. Look out ... it's behind you!

ON THE FENCE

Hmmmm ... OK, you'll admit some of it is quite hard to explain. But you're not going to just believe everything you hear, are you? You need some proper evidence—then you'll think about it. Very sensible!

FROM WOO TO TRUE

Some things start off as strange mysteries, but eventually scientists manage to make sense of them, and they become part of the explained, not the unexplained. For example, earthquake lights (see page 33) and ball lightning (see page 53) both used to be seen as made-up nonsense, but now we know they are real. Maybe that will happen with other things too, like haunted houses, alien abductions, or the Loch Ness monster!

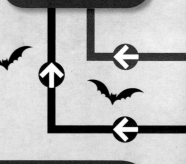

START HERE

WOULD YOU SPEND THE NIGHT IN A FAMOUS HAUNTED HOTEL?

YES → DO YOU HAVE LOTS OF WEIRD DREAMS?

NO ↓

ONLY IF I CAN SHARE A ROOM! →

YES ↓   **NO** ↓

ARE YOU SCARED OF THE DARK?

YES ←   **NO** →

DO YOU LIKE SCARY HORROR FILMS?

THEY'RE A BIT BORING.

NO ←   **YES** →

WHAT'S THE BEST EXPLANATION FOR UFOS?

ALIENS   AIRPLANES

HAS ANYONE YOU KNOW SEEN A GHOST?

YES ↓

SOME KIND OF NATURAL ENERGY.

DO YOU KNOW WHO'S CALLING WHEN YOU HEAR THE PHONE?

YES   **SOMETIMES**

THEY SAY THEY HAVE.

WHAT ARE GHOSTS?

YES ←   IF YOU VISITED LOCH NESS, WOULD YOU LOOK OUT FOR THE MONSTER?

NO ↓

THE WANDERING SOULS OF DEAD PEOPLE.

THERE AREN'T ANY GHOSTS!

SOME KIND OF UNEXPLAINED RECORDING OF PAST EVENTS.

IT'S ALL NONSENSE!
Harrumph! What kind of idiots actually believe in all this stuff anyway?! Well, you're not fooled—if there isn't a good, scientific explanation, you're not having any of it. So there. Paranormal, schmaranormal!

IT'S RAINING FISH AND FROGS

YOU'RE OUT FOR A NICE STROLL WHEN SUDDENLY ... PLOP! PLAP! SPLAT! Hundreds of fish are falling from the sky—crashing onto sidewalks, denting passing cars, and even landing on your head! Yep—it can happen. In fact, it's been happening for thousands of years ...

DON'T READ THIS BOOK BEFORE BED
0 1 2 3 4 5 6 7 8 9 10
FRIGHT-O-METER
UWILLBUPALL'S

A.D. 77, ROMAN ITALY
Roman author Pliny the Elder wrote a book called *Natural History* about nature, weather, and animals. In it, he said:

> *"There are sufficient modern proofs that living fishes, frogs, and other creatures or materials, have fallen in showers."*

A.D. 200, ANCIENT GREECE
Ancient Greek writer Heraclides Lembus described a heavy storm of frogs when he wrote:

> *"In Paeonia and Dardania it has, they say, before now rained frogs; and so great has been the number of these frogs that the houses and the roads have been full of them ..."*

1355, SOMEWHERE IN EUROPE
A rain of frogs was said to have taken place on this date. Not much is known about it, but it was later illustrated in this weird woodcut.

WILD WEATHER

DOZENS OF DEAD FISH LITTER A SIDEWALK.

SO IT REALLY CAN RAIN ANIMALS—AND NOT JUST FISH AND FROGS! WEIRD ANIMAL RAIN REPORTS ALSO INCLUDE TADPOLES AND JELLYFISH, TOADS, SNAILS, EELS, AND EVEN SNAKES AND SPIDERS. But although they have happened in many parts of the world, these strange showers tend to have several things in common.

➜ It's usually small, light animals that fall as "rain."

➜ They are often animals that live in water—fish are the most common.

➜ Each shower is normally of just one type of animal, such as fish, or frogs, or tadpoles.

➜ Animal rain often happens during, or just after, a more normal storm.

➜ Sometimes, the animals are frozen, or even broken up into pieces ...

➜ Other times they survive their ordeal and are still alive when they land.

1894, BATH, ENGLAND

A shower of small, gloopy, jellyfish-like things fell on the city of Bath, but it's not clear exactly what they were!

1947, LOUISIANA, U.S.A.

This freaky fish fall in Marksville, Louisiana, was seen by a wildlife scientist, Alexander Bajkov. He was having breakfast in a cafe when the strange rain began. He said:

"Automobiles and trucks were running over them ... Fish fell on the roofs of houses ... I personally collected ... a large jar of perfect specimens."

2009, ISHIKAWA, JAPAN

Several cities in this area of Japan experienced showers of tadpoles. They were described as making a strange sound as they fell!

2012, LAJAMANU, AUSTRALIA

When a shower of small fish called spangled perch fell onto the town of Lajamanu, people weren't all that surprised—it had happened at least twice before, in 2004 and 1974. But when people picked them up, they found the fish were still alive!

THE EXPLANATION

SO HOW COULD THIS HAPPEN? SCIENTISTS AND WEATHER EXPERTS THINK THEY HAVE AN ANSWER ...

THE LEADING THEORY IS THAT ANIMAL SHOWERS HAPPEN WHEN A SHOAL OF FISH, AN ARMY OF FROGS, OR CLUSTERS OF OTHER ANIMALS ARE SWEPT UP FROM A POND, RIVER, OR SEA (OR SOMETIMES FROM THE GROUND) BY A TORNADO. AT FIRST, PEOPLE THOUGHT WATERSPOUTS, WHICH ARE WHIRLWINDS OVER WATER, COULD DO THIS. BUT THEY ARE ACTUALLY NOT STRONG ENOUGH AND DON'T SUCK WATER UP. HOWEVER, A NORMAL TORNADO CAN PICK UP PEOPLE, HORSES, OR EVEN CARS, AND FLING THEM HIGH INTO THE AIR. SO WHEN A TORNADO PASSES OVER A RIVER OR AWAY FROM THE COAST AND OVER THE SEA, IT WOULD BE STRONG ENOUGH TO SUCK UP ANIMALS. THEN, AFTER BEING CARRIED SOME DISTANCE, THEY PLOP BACK DOWN AND LAND AT YOUR FEET.

THERE'S JUST ONE PROBLEM—AS FAR AS WE KNOW, NO ONE HAS EVER SEEN THE SUCKING-UP PART HAPPEN. BUT NO ONE HAS ANY BETTER IDEAS, EITHER! DO YOU?

PRESIDENTIAL POLTERGEISTS

ONE OF THE PERKS OF BEING PRESIDENT OF THE UNITED STATES IS THAT YOU GET TO LIVE IN THE FABULOUSLY GRAND AND SPACIOUS WHITE HOUSE, IN WASHINGTON, D.C. But you certainly won't be alone! In addition to the dozens of members of White House staff and security, family, and esteemed guests, this famous house plays host to a number of ghosts—including several previous presidents. They range from helpful and harmless to mean and menacing. Check out which wing is safe, and where you might want to bring a flashlight.

FRIGHT-O-METER
UWILLBEPALLN8
DON'T READ THIS BOOK BEFORE BED
0 1 2 3 4 5 6 7 8 9 10

ARTWORK SHOWING WILLIAM HENRY HARRISON ON HIS DEATHBED

THINGS
THAT GO BUMP ...

Several presidents and other residents and staff have heard strange noises coming from the White House attic. The spooky bumping and banging sounds are said to be made by none other than the ghost of William Henry Harrison, the ninth president. He took office in 1841 at the age of 68, and died of pneumonia just 32 days later. According to legend, the ruckus is caused by Harrison's ghost looking for something. If that's true, to this day he has never found it!

HELLO, DOLLEY!

Dolley Madison, the wife of the fourth president, James Madison, moved into the White House in 1809 and wasted no time fixing up the place. She was stylish, sociable, and brilliant at design. In addition to coming up with new decorating schemes, she created the White House's famous Rose Garden, and it's said her ghost remains there to this day.

Dolley doesn't normally bother anyone with her ghostly presence—it's said she just likes to keep an eye on her flowers, and sometimes wafts the perfume of roses around. But when a later First Lady, Ellen Wilson, decided to replace the Rose Garden, Dolley got mad! The gardeners who were sent to dig up the garden saw her ghost, and she scared them so much they refused to do it. Job well done, Dolley!

GRUPMY GHOST

White House residents and staff say they often hear a creepy, deep-voiced laugh coming from one of the rooms, the Rose Bedroom. It's said to be bad-tempered, foul-mouthed president Andrew Jackson, who was elected in 1828. He had furious arguments and even fights with his opponents, and his ghost is still in a terrible mood today. He's often heard stamping around the room and swearing.

WILLIE LINCOLN

IT'S THE THING

In 1911, when William Howard Taft was president, staff were haunted by a very creepy ghost that they named The Thing. According to them, The Thing was the ghost of a young boy, and used to come up behind the servants and press on their shoulders, terrifying them. The president was not impressed, and said he would fire anyone who spread gossip about the ghost. However, some people think The Thing was the ghost of Willie Lincoln, President Abraham Lincoln's son who died in the White House in 1862, at age 11.

THE WHITE HOUSE HAS 132 ROOMS, AND 35 OF THEM ARE BATHROOMS.

ABE'S APPARITION

Abraham Lincoln, who was president in the 1860s, is the best-known White House ghost of all. He's most often spotted in his favorite room—aptly named the Lincoln Bedroom. When British prime minister Winston Churchill visited in the 1940s, he stayed there. After getting out of his bath, he walked back into the room, and saw Lincoln standing by the fireplace!

President Ronald Reagan's daughter Maureen and her husband reportedly saw Lincoln in this bedroom, standing by the window. Even Reagan's pet dog was spooked by the Lincoln Bedroom.

The ghost is also said to pace up and down the second-floor corridors, knocking on doors in the night. When Queen Wilhelmina of the Netherlands was visiting, she described how she heard the knocking and opened the door. She saw Lincoln's ghost standing there, and fainted!

PECULIAR PREMONITION

ABRAHAM LINCOLN ALSO HAD A PRETTY SPOOKY EXPERIENCE HIMSELF, WHEN HE WAS ALIVE. ACCORDING TO HIS BODYGUARD WARD HILL LAMON, LINCOLN SAID THAT HE DREAMED THAT HE WALKED INTO A ROOM IN THE WHITE HOUSE TO FIND A FUNERAL GOING ON. WHEN HE ASKED WHO HAD DIED, HE WAS TOLD THAT IT WAS THE PRESIDENT, WHO HAD BEEN KILLED BY AN ASSASSIN.

A FEW DAYS AFTER THE DREAM, ON APRIL 14, 1865, LINCOLN WAS SHOT BY JOHN WILKES BOOTH WHILE SITTING IN THE AUDIENCE AT FORD'S THEATER. HE DIED THE NEXT DAY.

SPACE ODDITY

BLACK HOLE BASICS

YOUR SPACESHIP IS OUT OF CONTROL. IT'S CURVING THROUGH SPACE, CLOSER AND CLOSER TO AN ENORMOUS BLACK HOLE, AND IT'S TOO LATE TO ESCAPE.

As you scream in panic, you are dragged through the event horizon and into the darkness, to be crushed into nothingness and disappear forever ...

At least, that's what happens in sci-fi movies! Fortunately, up until now we've escaped this fate in reality. Not because black holes aren't real—they are! It's because they are much, much too far away for the spacecraft we have now to reach them.

So what is this space oddity, and better yet ... should we be frightened?

BLACK HOLES CAN FORM WHEN AN OLD STAR IN SPACE EXPLODES AND COLLAPSES IN ON ITSELF. THE MATERIAL THE STAR IS MADE FROM SCRUNCHES UP SO THAT IT'S VERY, VERY DENSE. That means there's a huge amount of stuff in a very small space.

The denser it gets, the more powerful its gravity, or pulling force, becomes. This just makes it collapse into a smaller and smaller space.

Eventually, all the stuff is squashed into a space that's SO tiny, it's just like a dot, or point. In fact, it's so itty-bitty, it basically takes up no space at all. That's right—it's basically NOT THERE. Yet it contains all the stuff that once made up a star the size of our sun, or even bigger.

This tiny dot, or point, is called a singularity.

FRIGHT-O-METER
DON'T READ THIS BOOK BEFORE BED
0 1 2 3 4 5 6 7 8 9 10
UWILL 1UPALLN8

AN IMAGE OF THE ENERGY AROUND A BLACK HOLE

EVENT HORIZON

BECAUSE IT IS SO DENSE, A BLACK HOLE HAS VERY, VERY STRONG GRAVITY. Anything that gets too close gets pulled into the black hole and into that tiny point, adding to how heavy and dense it is.

A black hole can pull in things like gas, dust, stars, and even light. Once light gets close enough, it gets pulled toward the middle and cannot be seen from the outside. Nor can anything else that falls in. That's why black holes are black!

Each black hole has an area around it where light disappears. The edge of this area is called the event horizon.

COMPUTER ARTWORK OF A SPIRAL GALAXY AND A BLACK HOLE

THE HOLE TRUTH

SINCE BLACK HOLES HAVE SUCH STRONG GRAVITY, PEOPLE OFTEN THINK THAT THEY WILL KEEP PULLING UNTIL ALL THE STARS, PLANETS, MOONS—AND EVERYTHING ELSE—GET SUCKED IN. But that's not true. Just like other massive space objects, like the sun or Earth, a black hole's gravity will only pull in things that are close enough. Things that are farther away may just orbit around the black hole, or not be affected by it. Unless, of course, our universe collided with another—which, according to the multiverse theory, is possible. So as long as a black hole is really far away—and they are!—there's no need to lose sleep worrying you'll get sucked in. Phew!

FINDING BLACK HOLES

INFORMATION OVERLOAD

IS YOUR BRAIN STARTING TO ACHE YET? It's not surprising—even scientists agree that black holes are extremely confusing, and in many ways, don't make any sense. How can a vast amount of stuff be squeezed into basically no space at all? It can only happen because in a black hole, the normal rules of science stop working.

BIGFOOT
CAUGHT ON CAMERA

WHAT IF THERE WERE HUGE, HAIRY HUMANLIKE CREATURES LIVING IN THE WORLD'S WILD FORESTS AND MOUNTAINS? NOT CHIMPS OR GORILLAS, AND NOT EXACTLY PEOPLE EITHER—BUT SOMETHING IN BETWEEN ...

Well, mysterious creatures like this have been reported around the world—in Asia, Australia, the Americas, and Europe. The most famous examples include the yeti, or Abominable Snowman, of the Himalaya; and the Sasquatch, or Bigfoot, often spotted in North America.

Strangely, despite numerous claims of sightings, we've never seen clear pictures of them, nor have we ever stumbled across the skeleton of one for scientists to study. Still, there are some people quite convinced that these ape-human hybrids are real, so bust out your magnifying glass and prepare to examine the most famous footage of all time.

DON'T READ THIS BOOK BEFORE BED

0 1 2 3 4 5 6 7 8 9 10

FRIGHT-O-METER

UWILLBUTALLN8

THIS PHOTO SHOWS THE FAMOUS "BIG-FOOT" CAUGHT ON CAMERA IN 1967.

INTO THE WOODS

The film was shot by a man named Roger Patterson, who had been interested in Bigfoot for years. He had talked to plenty of witnesses who had reported seeing the creature in the forests of Northern California.

So, in October 1967, Patterson set out on horseback with a friend, Bob Gimlin, to look for evidence. On October 27, according to Patterson, he and Gimlin passed by a fallen tree—then suddenly saw Bigfoot on the other side of a creek. Patterson jumped from his horse and grabbed his movie camera, then ran after the creature while trying to film it. The result is a shaky, blurry, but undeniable creepy Bigfoot video, lasting about 50 seconds.

So could this be a real film of an unknown humanoid creature, or is it a hoax?

SASQUATCH XING

THERE WOULD HAVE TO BE A POPULATION OF DOZENS OR HUNDREDS OF THESE CREATURES, SO THAT THEY COULD HAVE BABIES AND KEEP ON EXISTING. WHERE ARE THEY ALL HIDING?

MONKEYING AROUND?

For years, debate raged about whether the film was a fake, or proof that Bigfoot existed. Animal experts studied the film, and some of them thought it did show a real creature, still unknown to science. People also tried to re-create the film using a person in an ape suit—but it never looked quite right. Then, 30 years after the film was first shot, a friend of Patterson's named Bob Heironimus claimed that the Bigfoot was, in fact, him in a costume. He said he had agreed to wear a suit and play the part so that Patterson could film him. Not long after that, a costume-maker, Philip Morris, also came forward to say he had made an ape suit for Patterson.

Weirdly, though, the suits Morris and Heironimus described were very different, and their stories didn't match. Some people think they were faking it, in order to make money. It's odd that 30 years went by before they decided to say anything—and that witnesses at the time saw Patterson and Gimlin on their trip, but no third person.

Patterson died in 1972, but neither he nor Gimlin ever confessed to a hoax. The film remains a creepy and intriguing mystery ... and so does Bigfoot.

THE BIGFOOT FAMILY

MEET BIGFOOT'S RELATIVES FROM AROUND THE WORLD!

YETI, ABOMINABLE SNOWMAN, OR MEH-TEH (MEANING "MAN-BEAST")
- ➲ LOCATION: THE HIMALAYA MOUNTAIN RANGE, AND SIBERIA IN RUSSIA
- ➲ NOT ACTUALLY A SNOWMAN: LIKE BIGFOOT, THE YETI IS ACTUALLY A LARGE HUMANOID COVERED IN BLACK OR BROWN HAIR, SAID TO ROAM THE SNOWY LANDSCAPES OF PLACES LIKE NEPAL AND RUSSIA.

YOWIE
- ➲ LOCATION: AUSTRALIA
- ➲ THE AUSTRALIAN VERSION OF THE BIGFOOT IS A GINORMOUS, HAIRY, APELIKE CREATURE, SOMETIMES SAID TO STAND UP TO 12 FEET (3.6 M) TALL! YIKES!

ORANG PENDEK (MEANING "SHORT PERSON")
- ➲ LOCATION: INDONESIA IN SOUTHEAST ASIA
- ➲ UNLIKE THE OTHERS, THE ORANG PENDEK IS SAID TO BE SMALLER THAN AN AVERAGE HUMAN—ONLY ABOUT FOUR TO FIVE FEET (1.2 TO 1.5 M) TALL. LIKE THEM, THOUGH, IT IS COVERED IN BROWNISH HAIR AND WALKS UPRIGHT.

COULD A FOOTPRINT BE A CLUE?

HOW BIG IS BIGFOOT?

ACCORDING TO MOST SIGHTINGS, IT VARIES FROM ABOUT 6 FEET (1.8 M) TO 7.5 FEET (2.3 M) TALL—WITH FEET UP TO 16 INCHES (41 CM) LONG! IT'S ALSO SAID TO HAVE VERY LONG ARMS, A THICK BODY, AND A HUNCHED BACK.

WICKED WAVES

A TSUNAMI RUSHING TOWARD YOU IS ONE OF THE MOST TERRI-FYING SIGHTS ON EARTH. IT'S A ROARING WALL OF WATER, SURGING IN FROM THE SEA to smash into the coast and cover the land. If a tsunami strikes coastal towns and cities, it can destroy buildings, flatten farm-land, and cause thousands of casualties. And that's just a normal tsunami. A megatsunami is even bigger—and according to one scary scientific stat, it could be waiting to happen in the Atlantic Ocean.

A TSUNAMI IS BORN

A tsunami happens when something makes a large amount of seawater move suddenly. It could be a landslide, a volcanic eruption, or a big earthquake on the seafloor. The movement makes the sea surface move up and down, creating a massive ripple effect. It's like the ripples you see when you throw a stone into a pond, but a lot bigger. The ripples start to spread out across the sea, and travel toward the coast at high speed, in the form of large waves.

As they zoom across the ocean, the waves are low and very long. But as they move into shallower water near the shore, they pile up and pour onto the coast. A tsunami wave can flood far inland, as it is carrying so much seawater.

AFTER A DEADLY TSUNAMI IN JAPAN, A BOAT RESTS ON TOP OF A TWO-STORY BUILDING.

Wave

A tsunami hits a coast.

Epicenter of an earthquake

Tsunamis start during earthquakes. The giant waves travel across the sea.

STRIKE ZONE

Tsunamis are most common in the Pacific Ocean—they're a fairly familiar sight in places like Japan, Chile, and Hawaii, because there are a lot of earthquakes and volcanoes in those places. A terrible tsunami also struck Thailand and other parts of Asia in 2004, caused by a huge undersea earthquake near Indonesia.

Tsunamis aren't so common in the Atlantic Ocean—but that's exactly where one of the worst tsunamis ever could be waiting to happen.

DON'T READ THIS BOOK BEFORE BED
0 1 2 3 4 5 6 7 8 9 10
FRIGHT-O-METER
UWILLBUPALLNB

ILLUSTRATION OF A
MASSIVE TSUNAMI

CANARY
COLLAPSE

La Palma is one of the Canary Islands, located off the west coat of Africa. It's home to a volcano called Cumbre Vieja. In 2001, two scientists suggested that a huge chunk of land on the west side of Cumbre Vieja was loose and at risk of moving. If there was a volcanic eruption or earthquake, it could suddenly slip downhill in a giant landslide, and plunge into the sea.

This would cause a massive megatsunami, with waves up to 300 feet (91 m) high crashing over nearby islands. By the time the ripples spread out around the Atlantic Ocean, the tsunami waves could still be more than 150 feet (46 m) tall. They would crash into the Caribbean, South America, and the East Coast of the United States—where there are a lot of population-packed towns and cities.

DUE TO CLIMATE CHANGE, SEA LEVELS WORLDWIDE ARE GRADUALLY RISING BECAUSE OF MELTING ICE AROUND THE NORTH AND SOUTH POLES. THIS MEANS TSUNAMIS COULD BE EVEN MORE DANGEROUS, AS IT WILL BE EASIER FOR THE SEA TO FLOOD ONTO THE LAND.

TSUNAMI
SAFETY

JUST IN CASE YOU ARE EVER CAUGHT UP IN A TSUNAMI, THOUGH, IT'S A GOOD IDEA TO BE PREPARED. WATCH OUT FOR THESE WARNING SIGNS AND REMEMBER OUR SAFETY TIPS!

TSUNAMI WARNING SIGNS:
- ➲ IF THE SEA SUDDENLY GETS SUCKED AWAY OFF THE BEACH, IT CAN MEAN A BIG TSUNAMI WAVE IS COMING.
- ➲ ALTERNATIVELY, YOU MIGHT SEE A WAVE COMING, OR THE SEA STARTING TO RISE SUDDENLY.
- ➲ IF YOU FEEL AN EARTHQUAKE WHEN YOU'RE CLOSE TO THE COAST, BE PREPARED FOR A TSUNAMI.
- ➲ TSUNAMI AREAS OFTEN HAVE TSUNAMI WARNING SIRENS TOO— DON'T IGNORE THEM!

WHAT TO DO:
- ➲ DON'T STAY TO WATCH! GET AWAY BEFORE IT'S TOO LATE.
- ➲ HEAD INLAND AND AIM FOR HIGH GROUND SUCH AS A HILLTOP.
- ➲ IF THAT'S NOT POSSIBLE, CLIMB A TREE OR GO INTO A STRONG BUILDING AND GO UP SEVERAL FLOORS.
- ➲ DON'T GO BACK WHEN THE TSUNAMI HAS PASSED, AS THERE CAN BE SEVERAL TSUNAMI WAVES ONE AFTER ANOTHER. WAIT TO BE RESCUED.

TSUNAMI HAZARD ZONE

IN CASE OF EARTHQUAKE GO TO HIGH GROUND OR INLAND

REMAIN
CALM

In other words, whole cities would be ruined, and thousands or millions of lives would be at stake. But before you go inflating inner tubes, some people think this theory is far-fetched! When the idea was first suggested, it caused a panic. But since then, quite a few other scientists have disagreed, saying they don't think the landslide would be that big after all, and probably wouldn't cause a major disaster. Let's hope they're right!

BEEN THERE, DONE THAT

Here B4

HAS THIS HAPPENED TO YOU? FOR JUST A FEW SECONDS, WHEN SOMETHING TOTALLY NORMAL IS GOING ON, YOU SUDDENLY GET THE CREEPIEST FEELING THAT IT'S NOT THE FIRST TIME IT HAS HAPPENED. Turning a corner and seeing that doorway ... hearing that music in the distance ... and then that orange truck driving past. You knew it was going to happen that way—just like last time! So what exactly is the freaky phenomenon known as déjà vu?

The term "déjà vu" is French, and means "already seen." And that's just how it feels. You get a strong sense that something has happened

before, even when you know that's not possible. It could be when you're in a new place you've never visited before, or having a conversation with someone you've never met before—but you get a strange, overwhelming sense of familiarity.

Maybe you're thinking, "Uh? What are you talking about?" In that case, déjà vu has probably never happened to you. But if it has, you'll recognize the superweird feeling of going through your life for a second time, just for a few brief moments.

DON'T READ THIS BOOK BEFORE BED

0 1 2 3 4 5 6 7 8 9 10

FRIGHT-O-METER

UWIL...BUPALLN8

FEEL LIKE YOU'VE BEEN HERE BEFORE? YOU HAVE!

BRAIN BLIP

DÉJÀ VU IS A BIT OF A MYSTERY, LIKE A LOT OF THINGS HAVING TO DO WITH THE HUMAN BRAIN. But scientists have come up with several theories about how it works, and they all have to do with a brief brain blip:

THEORY 1: MEMORY MISTAKE

According to this theory, you're simply mismatching what's happening now to a memory from the past. The old memory could be similar in some ways, so your brain makes a mistake and thinks the same thing happened twice.

THEORY 2: BRAIN SIDES

The two sides of your brain are mainly separate, but linked by bundles of nerves. Sometimes, one side could pass information to the other, when it already has it. You would sense getting the information once, then again a split second later as the message arrived from the other side. You might experience this as something feeling familiar.

THEORY 3: BRAIN GLITCH

Scientists have found that an electrical signal in one part of the brain tells you when you've seen something before, so you can "jog your memory." But maybe this sometimes happens by mistake. This would give you a sense of recognition, even when it was impossible.

DÉJÀ VU AND EPILEPSY

SOME PEOPLE HAVE A BRAIN CONDITION CALLED TEMPORAL LOBE EPILEPSY. The electrical signals in their brains can go haywire, making them have seizures. During a seizure, they experience strange sensations, or cannot move normally.

Epilepsy sufferers often say that just before a seizure, they get a really strong sense of déjà vu. That makes it seem likely that it is caused by something going wrong with your brain's electrical system—like what happens in a seizure, but not as severe.

THERE IS NO "NOW"

AS WE GO ABOUT OUR DAILY LIVES, WE HAVE A STRONG SENSE OF WHAT IS HAPPENING IN THE HERE AND NOW. YOUR BRAIN TELLS YOU WHERE YOU ARE, WHAT YOU'RE DOING, WHAT THAT BANANA YOU'RE EATING TASTES LIKE, AND SO ON.

BUT SCIENTISTS WHO STUDY THE BRAIN SAY THAT SENSE OF "RIGHT NOW" IS REALLY JUST AN ILLUSION. IT TAKES A LITTLE TIME—SOME SAY AS MUCH AS SEVERAL SECONDS—FOR YOUR BRAIN TO PROCESS WHAT'S GOING ON AROUND YOU, MAKE SENSE OF IT, AND "TELL" YOU WHAT YOU ARE EXPERIENCING AND WHAT IT MEANS. BY THE TIME YOU EXPERIENCE "NOW," IT'S ALREADY HAPPENED!

TOTAL RECALL

ON THE OTHER HAND, PEOPLE WHO BELIEVE IN REINCARNATION (SEE PAGES 96–97) HAVE OTHER IDEAS.

They say déjà vu means you probably are remembering something you've seen before—in a past life! Or it could be triggered by meeting someone who you met or knew in a previous life. A slightly spookier explanation for sure, but could it possibly be true?

UNDER YOUR SKIN

FEELING ITCHY? WELL, YOU DEFINITELY WILL BE, once you've read about these scary skin-dwellers! You may have heard of creepy-crawly parasites that like to scuttle over your skin, biting you to suck your blood. But did you know there's something even worse? We're not talking about lice and bugs that like to live on your skin. Check out these creepy critters that want to live IN it!

DON'T READ THIS BOOK BEFORE BED

0 1 2 3 4 5 6 7 8 9 10

FRIGHT-O-METER

UWILLBUPALL'8

THE LARVA EVEN HAS SHARP SPINES TO MAKE IT REALLY HARD TO PULL OUT.

BURROWING BOTWORM

Maggots are revolting enough wherever they are—but imagine having a big, fat maggot living right under your skin! This happens if you get infected by a botfly.

First, the cunning mother fly lays her eggs on a bloodsucking tick. If the tick bites you, a maggot—that is, a larva, or baby fly—can climb off the tick and onto your skin. It burrows into the skin and stays there for EIGHT WEEKS, feeding on your flesh and growing bigger and bigger. It also creates a sore bump on your skin, called a warble.

Finally, the baby botfly wriggles out of its hole, and drops into the soil, in order to pupate and hatch out into an adult fly. But you'll want it out before that, because having a munching, growing botfly larva stuck into you really hurts!

You can't squeeze it out, as this can cause it to pop and release its insides into you, making you really ill. Instead, a doctor has to carefully pluck it out with tweezers.

ONE **PERSON** HAD A BOTFLY LARVA REMOVED FROM THEIR EYE.

A FULLY REMOVED WORM!

IN THE PROCESS OF REMOVING THE GUINEA WORM

GRUESOME
GUINEA WORM

You're probably thinking it can't possibly get any creepier. Well, you haven't met the guinea worm, which lays its eggs in water. The larvae hatch and get swallowed by water fleas (but stay alive inside them). If you drink water that has a water flea in it, the flea dies in your stomach, and the baby guinea worm escapes.

Then the worm grows, and grows, and grows inside your body, reaching up to three feet (1 m) long! Finally, it needs to get out, in order to lay more eggs. It starts to emerge from your body, often from your foot or leg. Where it comes out, it causes an agonizing burning pain that makes you want to stick your leg in cold water. Then the worm releases its eggs into the water, and the cycle starts all over again!

Left to itself, the worm comes out very slowly. To speed it up, the traditional method is to wind it around a stick or a pencil, and pull a little more out each day. You must be careful not to break the worm, though, or part of it will be left inside you! It can take weeks to get a worm out, and it's horribly painful.

THE ANCIENT EGYPTIANS USED THIS METHOD TO GET A GUINEA WORM OUT AROUND 3,500 YEARS AGO.

GOODBYE, WORMS!

THE GOOD NEWS IS, THESE DISGUSTING CREATURES ARE NOT COMMON IN MOST COUNTRIES, SO YOU PROBABLY DON'T HAVE TO WORRY ABOUT ONE GETTING INTO YOU. IN FACT, GUINEA WORMS HAVE BEEN PRETTY MUCH WIPED OUT BY A BIG CHARITY CAMPAIGN. GOOD RIDDANCE!

MYSTERIOUS
MORGELLONS

MANY PEOPLE SAY THEY HAVE A STRANGE SKIN DISEASE KNOWN AS MORGELLONS, WHICH DATES BACK TO MEDIEVAL TIMES. IT CAUSES ITCHY, PAINFUL SORES THAT OFTEN SEEM TO HAVE TINY THREADLIKE THINGS GROWING OUT FROM UNDER THE SKIN. MANY DOCTORS AND SCIENTISTS, HOWEVER, THINK MORGELLONS ISN'T REAL. THEY SAY THE THREADS JUST COME FROM BANDAGES OR CLOTHES, AND THAT PEOPLE ARE IMAGINING THE ITCHING AND CAUSING THE SORES BY SCRATCHING. IT IS POSSIBLE FOR PEOPLE TO IMAGINE THEY HAVE PARASITES IN THEIR SKIN WHEN THERE IS NOTHING REALLY THERE. THIS IS CALLED DELUSIONAL PARASITOSIS, AND IT'S QUITE COMMON. BUT THEN WHERE ARE THE STRANGE THREADS COMING FROM?

MORGELLONS SUFFERERS SAY THE THREADS COULD BE CAUSED BY A TYPE OF BACTERIA CALLED SPIROCHETES, AND THAT YOU CAN CATCH MORGELLONS FROM SOMEONE WHO HAS IT. DOCTORS AND PATIENTS ARE STILL DEBATING THE TRUTH.

THE GREEN CHILDREN OF WOOLPIT

IF YOU GO TO THE VILLAGE OF WOOLPIT IN SUFFOLK, ENGLAND, YOU'LL FIND IT HAS A STRANGE WELCOME SIGN. On it there's a wolf, and two green children. What's the significance? Recording the town's history, of course! Even though it happened 900 years ago, the village has never forgotten about the time when two strange children with green clothes and skin appeared out of nowhere, speaking an unknown language.

Were they fairies? Or maybe aliens? Travelers from a strange, dark world, as they claimed? Or is the story just an old folktale? Two history writers who lived at around that time, Ralph of Coggeshall and William of Newburgh, both recorded the events at Woolpit as fact, not fiction.

AT THE WOLF PITS

THE VILLAGE WAS NAMED WOOLPIT AFTER ITS WOLF PITS— TRENCHES DUG AS TRAPS TO CATCH WOLVES (WHICH LIVED IN ENGLAND LONG AGO). Some time in the mid-1100s, during the harvest, people working near the wolf pits came across two small children, an older girl and a younger boy. They were wandering around the pits seeming lost and frightened.

The first thing they noticed was that the children were green! Their clothes were green, their eyes were green, and so was their skin. They were oddly dressed, in fabrics the villagers had never seen before. They also spoke an unknown language, and no one could understand them.

FRIGHT-O-METER
DON'T READ THIS BOOK BEFORE BED
0 1 2 3 4 5 6 7 8 9 10
UWILLBUPALLNS

GREEN SKIN, GREEN FOOD?

THE CHILDREN WERE TAKEN TO THE HOME OF WEALTHY SIR RICHARD DE CALNE, TO BE CARED FOR BY HIS SERVANTS. At first, even though they seemed hungry, they wouldn't eat any of the food they were offered. At last, someone brought some fresh green beans to the house, and the children tore the pods open and ate the beans inside.

Over time, they began to eat other foods too, and gradually, they became less green. But the boy always seemed sad and lonely, and after a while, he died. The girl, however, survived, and was named Agnes. Eventually, she learned to speak English—and once she could, she told a very strange story.

THE UNDERGROUND LAND

Agnes described how she and her brother had once lived in a place called St Martin's Land, which was separated from other lands by a big river. It was never sunny there, but always gloomy, and all the people were green. One day, the children were looking after their family's cattle when they got lost and went into a cave. They heard a loud sound and saw a flash of light, then emerged into Woolpit village. They were amazed and terrified by how bright it was, and how different it was from their home. But then the villagers found them, and they could not go back.

As the story has been told over time, people have developed a number of theories about where the green children of Woolpit might have actually come from:

ELVES FROM UNDERGROUND

Several Scandinavian countries have legends about elves or fairy folk who live underground, or in rocks. Was this the "dark land" the children had come from?

POISONED ORPHANS

The story has been linked to another local legend, the Babes in the Wood. In this story, a rich man dies and leaves his two children to be brought up by his brother. But the brother wants them dead, so he can take their money. They end up abandoned in a forest. Were the green children the original Babes in the Wood? One suggestion is that they were poisoned with arsenic, which can give the skin a green tint.

ALIENS

Aliens are green, right? (At least by some reports!) So some people think the green children actually came from another planet—a dark and gloomy one—perhaps by teleportation.

A REASONABLE EXPLANATION?

THOUGH IT'S NOT QUITE AS EXCITING, THERE COULD BE ANOTHER EXPLANATION. THE CHILDREN COULD HAVE BEEN IMMIGRANTS FROM FLANDERS, IN EUROPE—THIS WAS COMMON IN SUFFOLK IN THE 1100S. THAT WOULD EXPLAIN THEIR STRANGE LANGUAGE AND CLOTHES. A POOR DIET COULD HAVE GIVEN THEM AN ILLNESS CALLED GREEN SICKNESS, MAKING THEIR SKIN LOOK GREENISH. THEY MIGHT HAVE BEEN LIVING IN THE NEARBY TOWN OF FORNHAM ST. MARTIN. WHEN THEY BECAME SEPARATED FROM THEIR PARENTS AND GOT LOST. OVER TIME, THE STORY COULD HAVE BEEN EXAGGERATED, AND TURNED INTO A CREEPY LEGEND.

THE GHOSTS OF FLIGHT 401

THE GHOSTS IN THIS STORY ARE PRETTY UNUSUAL FOR SEVERAL REASONS: THEY APPEARED ON AIRPLANES, RATHER THAN IN ANCIENT CASTLES OR SPOOKY CELLARS. They weren't out to spook people—they just wanted to be helpful! And finally, these ghosts were seen by so many reliable witnesses, they make for one of the most convincing ghost stories ever.

DON'T READ THIS BOOK BEFORE BED

0 1 2 3 4 5 6 7 8 9 10

FRIGHT-O-METER

UWILLBUPILLN8

WRECKAGE IN THE SWAMP

The story begins with a disastrous airplane crash in the Everglades near Miami, Florida, U.S.A., on December 29, 1972. Eastern Air Lines Flight 401 from New York was meant to be landing in Miami. But there was a problem—an indicator light wasn't working, and the pilots couldn't tell if the landing gear was properly in place. As they circled around trying to fix it, they didn't notice that the plane was slowly losing altitude. By the time they did, it was too late.

As the plane crashed in the swampy Everglades, the mud and water absorbed some of the impact, giving it a relatively soft landing. As a result, 75 people survived. But Captain Bob Loft and flight engineer Don Repo were among those who did not.

AIRBOATS!

AIRBOATS, A POPULAR TYPE OF BOAT FOR SIGHTSEEING AND SPOTTING ALLIGATORS IN THE EVERGLADES, WERE SENT TO HELP RESCUE SURVIVORS AFTER THE CRASH OF FLIGHT 401.

THE SAME TYPE OF PLANE AS FLIGHT 401—A LOCKHEED TRISTAR L-1011

THE GHOSTS APPEAR

It was the following year, 1973, when people on board other Tristar airliners began to report strange and spooky sightings. The witnesses included passengers, crew, and even senior airline managers.

One executive boarded his plane and headed for first class. He was surprised to see a pilot in full uniform standing in the cabin. He went over to have a chat—then realized that he recognized who it was. It was Captain Bob Loft! Moments later, the captain vanished, and the alarmed exec spoke to the crew and had the plane searched. There was no sign of anyone.

The same thing happened to the cabin crew on board another flight. They saw a captain in the cabin and even chatted to him, before he suddenly disappeared right in front of them. The crew was so shocked, the flight had to be canceled.

A flight engineer—the same job Don Repo had done—came to do the preflight check on another Tristar. But he found Don Repo, who he recognized immediately, sitting in the cockpit. Repo said, "You don't need to worry about the preflight, I've already done it"—and was gone.

Two women on separate flights saw a strange, uniformed man sitting near them, and called the staff to say that he seemed quiet or unwell. Each time, the man then vanished, as passengers and crew watched. When the women were later shown pictures of the crew of Flight 401, they identified the man as Don Repo.

AN AIRPLANE GALLEY

THE GOOD GHOST

One flight attendant had an especially big shock when she opened an oven in a Tristar galley, or kitchen, and saw Don Repo looking out at her from inside! She quickly called another attendant, who saw the face too. Then Repo said: "Watch out for fire on this plane." The plane later had to be grounded after its engine malfunctioned—luckily, it didn't catch fire or crash.

HAUNTED PLANE PARTS

THE SPOOKIEST THING ABOUT THIS HAUNTING IS THAT THE GHOSTS WERE SEEN ON BOARD TRISTARS FITTED WITH REUSED PARTS FROM CRASHED FLIGHT 401. IT WAS AS IF LOFT AND REPO HAD COME WITH THEM! THE GALLEY KITCHEN WHERE REPO GAVE HIS WARNING WAS ONE OF THE PARTS THAT HAD BEEN REUSED.

THOUGH PLENTY OF ITS STAFF REPORTED SEEING THE GHOSTS, EASTERN AIR LINES DID NOT WANT PEOPLE TO THINK ITS PLANES WERE HAUNTED AND TRIED TO COVER UP THE STORY. HOWEVER, IT'S SAID THAT THE COMPANY DID EVENTUALLY REMOVE ALL THE SALVAGED PARTS, JUST IN CASE. AFTER THAT, THE HAUNTINGS APPARENTLY STOPPED.

LITTLE FORGOTTEN PLACE

FORGOTTEN PLACE

FRIGHT-O-METER

DON'T READ THIS BOOK BEFORE BED

0 1 2 3 4 5 6 7 8 9 10

UWILLBUPALLNS

"THROW HIM IN THE DUNGEONS!" THAT'S THE LAST THING YOU'D WANT TO HEAR IF YOU WERE AN ENEMY HELD CAPTIVE IN A MEDIEVAL EUROPEAN CASTLE. These towering fortresses are famous for their deep, dark prison cells, where miserable captives were left to starve, or go mad.

All dungeons in those days were pretty scary, especially if you were the unfortunate prisoner thrown inside. Usually just a bare stone room, often deep in the basement or underground, they were horribly dark, damp, cold, and dirty. Water might drip from the ceiling or leak in through the walls. There could be some rusty iron shackles, or a ball and chain. And you'd get to share your new home with rats, spiders, and maybe even the old, moldy skeletons of previous residents.

DUNGEON OF DOOM

The worst type of dungeon of them all was the dreaded oubliette. An oubliette is a dungeon that has no doors. The only way to get in (or out, if you're lucky enough) is through a small hatch or circular hole in the ceiling. It's way too high to try to climb out of, so you can only escape using a ladder or a rope (if someone is nice enough to bring you one), that is).

If the guards wanted to keep you alive, they would lower some stinky water and stale bread down through the hole once in a while. If they didn't ... you were DOOMED. Some prisoners were kept in the oubliette for just a short time to give them a fright, or were held there before being put on trial. But others were dumped down the hole and forgotten, to die a slow, agonizing death.

In fact, the name oubliette is French for "little forgotten place." In other words, it was the dungeon where they put you if they never wanted to bother with you again ...

ETCHING OF A DUNGEON IN THE TOWER OF LONDON

DUNGEON DESIGNS

Some oubliettes were large, like a standard dungeon, but others were tiny—just big enough to hold one person, often in an uncomfortable standing position. Stuck in that terrifyingly claustrophobic space, with no hope of getting out, prisoners often lost their minds.

Check out these real oubliettes that can still be seen today in old castles (don't worry, they haven't been in use in quite some time).

One of the oldest oubliettes is in Château de Pierrefonds, in France, where oubliettes were invented.

Conisbrough Castle in England has its oubliette at the bottom of its thick-walled central tower, or keep.

Many Scottish castles have a type of oubliette called a bottle dungeon. It's shaped like a bottle, with sloping roof leading up to the round opening at the top.

CONISBROUGH

BOTTLE DUNGEON

THE OUBLIETTE AT PIERREFONDS

CREEPY LEAP CASTLE

PERHAPS THE SCARIEST OUBLIETTE OF ALL IS AT LEAP CASTLE IN IRELAND, SAID TO BE ONE OF THE MOST CHILLING AND HAUNTED CASTLES ANYWHERE IN THE WORLD. FOR CENTURIES IT WAS OWNED BY THE TERRIFYING O'CARROLL FAMILY, WHO WERE FAMOUS FOR MERCILESSLY MURDERING ANYONE THEY DIDN'T LIKE.

THE CASTLE HAS A CHAPEL THAT PEOPLE SAY IS HORRIBLY HAUNTED, EVER SINCE ONE OF THE O'CARROLL FAMILY STABBED HIS OWN BROTHER TO DEATH THERE. IN THE CORNER OF THE CHAPEL IS A DOORWAY THAT LEADS TO A TRAP DOOR, AND BELOW THIS IS A DEEP, SPOOKY OUBLIETTE. PERHAPS THE O'CARROLLS PUSHED PEOPLE DOWN THERE WHEN THEY WANTED TO GET RID OF THEM!

IN THE EARLY 1900S, A NEW FAMILY, THE DARBYS, HAD TAKEN OVER THE CASTLE, AND THEY DECIDED TO HAVE THE OLD OUBLIETTE CLEARED OUT. TO THEIR HORROR, THE WORKMEN DOING THE JOB FOUND PILES AND PILES OF SKELETONS IN THE BOTTOM, LYING AMONG AND ON TOP OF A SET OF WOODEN SPIKES. ANYONE WHO FELL INTO THIS OUBLIETTE WAS NOT MEANT TO COME OUT ALIVE!

HA

LICKING STONES!

IN THE DUNGEON OF CARLISLE CASTLE IN ENGLAND, THERE ARE SMOOTH "LICKING STONES." THIS WAS WHERE DESPERATELY THIRSTY PRISONERS USED TO LICK THE DAMP WALL TO TRY TO SLURP UP SOME MOISTURE.

MONGOLIAN DEATH WORM

IF YOU VISIT MONGOLIA'S VAST, INHOSPITABLE GOBI DESERT, MAKE SURE YOU LOOK WHERE YOU'RE GOING! If you're not careful, you could accidentally step on a Mongolian death worm. And that would be the end of you—as it would most certainly zap you with a killer electric shock, squirt you with its deadly acidic venom, or possibly both!

FRIGHT-O-METER

DON'T READ THIS BOOK BEFORE BED

0 1 2 3 4 5 6 7 8 9 10

UWILLBLPALLNG

ACCORDING TO LOCALS, THE DEATH WORM IS ESPECIALLY ATTRACTED TO THE COLOR YELLOW. SO MAYBE YOU'D BETTER LEAVE YOUR FAVORITE YELLOW SOCKS AT HOME.

WICKED WORM

On the other hand, you might escape alive, as there's no proof so far that the Mongolian death worm actually exists. It's a cryptid—a creature that people have reported seeing, but which has still not been scientifically discovered or documented.

Yet to people who live in this area, the death worm is a real thing, known in the Mongolian language as the *olgoi-khorkhoi*. Most Mongolians will tell you that they've either seen one, know someone who has, or have seen animals such as camels that the death worm has killed. People are really scared of the worm, and say that simply touching one can be lethal.

A SPECIES OF SKINK CALLED A SANDFISH THAT "SWIMS" THROUGH SAND

MARTIAN MENACES?

According to the many reports about it, the Mongolian death worm is pretty weird—perhaps even stranger than all other legendary creatures. Most cryptids are said to look like humans, wild animals, or even dinosaurs. But the death worm really does sound like a creature from outer space—unlike any other living animal we know of.

DRAWING OF THE MONGOLIAN DEATH WORM

THE SEARCH IS ON

Many explorers, scientists, and photographers from outside Mongolia have gone to look for the death worm, or to try to find out more about it. None of them have ever managed to find one, catch one, or take a good photo. However, they often come away believing the worm does really exist, because the local people they speak to are so convinced of it. They think of the death worm as you might think of a bear—scary and dangerous, but definitely not a myth.

WORM-HUNTING 101

If you want to search for the death worm, you'll need to know its key features. Use our handy field guide to make sure you know it when you see it!

- Length: From two to five feet (0.6 to 1.5 m) long
- Color: Red, with darker blotches
- Shaped like a sausage
- Soft, wrinkled skin
- Spiky horns or teeth at one end—or, according to some reports, both ends
- Can spit or squirt strong acid at its enemies, which turns them yellow and rots their skin
- Can also deliver a powerful electric shock, which can kill a human or a camel
- Often found close to the saxaul plant
- Burrows and wriggles along under the sand, making wavelike patterns appear on the surface

IS THERE REALLY A DEATH WORM?

COULD AN ANIMAL LIKE THIS REALLY EXIST? WELL, ALTHOUGH IT DOES SOUND INCREDIBLY STRANGE, SOME OF THE DEATH WORM'S ABILITIES AND FEATURES ARE SEEN IN OTHER ANIMALS—JUST NOT ALL TOGETHER IN ONE PACKAGE. SPITTING COBRAS CAN SPIT VENOM SEVERAL FEET, WITH GREAT ACCURACY. LIZARDS CALLED SANDFISH CAN BURROW ALONG AT HIGH SPEED UNDER THE SAND, AND ELECTRIC EELS AND RAYS CAN GIVE YOU A POWERFUL ELECTRIC SHOCK. SO THESE ABILITIES DEFINITELY AREN'T IMPOSSIBLE.

SOME EXPERTS THINK THE DEATH WORM COULD PERHAPS BE AN UNKNOWN TYPE OF SNAKE OR LIZARD—OR MAYBE SOME KIND OF INVERTEBRATE, SUCH AS A MILLIPEDE OR VELVET WORM.

THERE CERTAINLY COULD BE AN UNDISCOVERED ANIMAL LIVING IN THE GOBI DESERT, AS IT'S A VERY BIG, REMOTE PLACE. IF THE WORM HIDES IN BURROWS, AS THE LOCALS SAY, THAT COULD BE WHY IT'S HARD TO SPOT.

BUT PEOPLE ALSO TEND TO EXAGGERATE STORIES ABOUT STRANGE CREATURES LIKE THESE. IF SCIENTISTS EVER DO FIND THE DEATH WORM, IT MIGHT BE SMALLER AND LESS DEADLY THAN ITS REPUTATION SUGGESTS.

THE NAME *OLGOI-KHORKHOI* IS MONGOLIAN FOR "LARGE INTESTINE WORM," AS THE WORM IS SAID TO LOOK LIKE A COW'S INTESTINE.

QUIZ
MYSTERIES OF SCIENCE

YOU MIGHT THINK SCIENCE IS THE OPPOSITE OF THE PARANORMAL. **Scientists look for evidence to help explain and prove things.** Ghosts, lake monsters, telepathy, and other unexplained events haven't been proved once and for all, **so they are not seen as scientific "truth". But did you know that for all science has taught us, there are still some pretty weird mysteries we're trying to figure out? Especially when we try to answer the really BIG questions, like what matter is made of, how time works, and how our brains think. Take this mysterious science quiz, and see if you can get to the bottom of some of the mysteries of science!**

2 **WHICH OF THESE THINGS IS STILL A MYSTERY FOR SCIENTISTS?**

A. Where bees go in winter
B. How spiders spin webs
C. How cats purr
D. Why your fingertips wrinkle up in the bath

3 **WHICH EVERYDAY HUMAN BEHAVIOR HAS NOT BEEN FULLY EXPLAINED?**

A. Laughing
B. Swallowing
C. Belching
D. Yawning

1 **WHAT DO SCIENTISTS THINK EVERYTHING IS MADE OF?**

A. Tiny strings
B. Tiny doughnuts
C. Tiny balls
D. Tiny discs

4 **SCIENTISTS DON'T KNOW HOW ONE OF THE ANIMALS IN RUSSIA'S LAKE BAIKAL GOT THERE. WHICH IS IT?**

A. The golomyanka, a weird transparent fish
B. The Baikal sturgeon, a large fish
C. The nerpa, a type of small seal
D. The strange green Lake Baikal sponge

5 WHAT WILL EVERYTHING IN THE UNIVERSE END UP AS?

A. Water   B. Heat   C. Dust   D. Soil

6 IF YOU WERE GIVEN A FAKE MEDICINE FOR A HEADACHE, DO YOU THINK IT WOULD WORK?

A. Yes, it would probably help you.
B. Only if you didn't know it was fake.
C. No, a fake medicine can't do anything.
D. Your headache might go away, but that would have happened anyway.

7 WHY DOES THE MOON LOOK BIGGER WHEN IT'S NEARER TO THE HORIZON?

A. Because it is bigger when it's there
B. Because you compare it to small objects on the horizon
C. Because you expect things on the horizon to be far away and look small, so the moon seems too big
D. Because it is magnified by Earth's atmosphere

ANSWERS:

1. WHAT DO SCIENTISTS THINK EVERYTHING IS MADE OF?
A. Tiny strings. The matter, or stuff, around us is made of tiny units called atoms, and atoms themselves are made of even tinier particles. But what are they made of? One of the leading theories says that all stuff is in fact made of minuscule, vibrating string shapes. Actually, though, this is just one idea of several, and nobody really knows for sure.

2. WHICH OF THESE THINGS IS STILL A MYSTERY FOR SCIENTISTS?
C. How cats purr. We know that purring happens in a cat's throat, and that cats do it when they're happy. But scientists have not found any "purring organ," and they aren't sure exactly what makes the sound—or how it's helpful to cats to purr when they're happy!

3. WHICH EVERYDAY HUMAN BEHAVIOR HAS NOT BEEN FULLY EXPLAINED?
D. Yawning. Scientists aren't sure why we yawn, though they have several ideas: to get more oxygen into the brain, to cool the brain down to help us stay alert, or even to show off our teeth! Yawning is "contagious," and this may be because in prehistoric times, this could help a group of people stay awake (so they could watch out for dangers, such as saber-toothed cats).

4. SCIENTISTS DON'T KNOW HOW ONE OF THE ANIMALS IN RUSSIA'S LAKE BAIKAL GOT THERE. WHICH IS IT?
C. The nerpa, a type of small seal. Lake Baikal's cute nerpa seal is the only freshwater seal in the world—that is, the only seal that lives in an inland lake, instead of in the salty seas. Lake Baikal, in Russia, is so far from the sea that it's a mystery how seals got there.

5. WHAT WILL EVERYTHING IN THE UNIVERSE END UP AS?
B. Heat. This is a confusing one! As time goes on, everything in the universe gets more disordered and mixed up, and all forms of energy ultimately end up as heat. This is known as entropy. If the universe carries on as it is now, then in the end—unimaginably far into the future—there will just be heat left, well, according to some scientists, anyway!

6. IF YOU WERE GIVEN A FAKE MEDICINE FOR A HEADACHE, DO YOU THINK IT WOULD WORK?
A. Yes, it would probably help you. In lab tests, when people are given fake pills or injections that contain no real medicine (called placebos), they still have a positive effect—for example, reducing headaches or back pain. This is called the placebo effect. Weirdly, it still works even when people KNOW they are getting a placebo! Somehow, giving the "medicine" helps the body fix the problem itself. Scientists don't know how or why the placebo effect works.

7. WHY DOES THE MOON LOOK BIGGER WHEN IT'S NEARER TO THE HORIZON?
Probably B or C, or both. B. Because you compare it to small objects on the horizon. C. Because you expect things on the horizon to be far away and look small, so the moon seems too big. Wherever the moon is in the sky, it actually takes up the same amount of your field of vision and is the same size. If you took a photo of it when it is high above and a photo of it near the horizon, the photos would show two matching moons. But it looks much bigger to our eyes when it's down low. Experts argue about the reasons why, but the two theories above are the most popular.

SWALLOWED UP!

FRIGHT-O-METER
UWILLBUPALLNB

THE GREAT BLUE HOLE IN BELIZE IS A SINKHOLE UNDER THE SEA. WHERE THE SINKHOLE IS, THE WATER IS MUCH DEEPER AND DARKER.

WHEN PEOPLE ARE TALKING ABOUT A TIME WHEN THEY FELT EMBARRASSED, THEY SOMETIMES SAY, "I JUST WANTED THE GROUND TO OPEN UP AND SWALLOW ME!" Of course, no one really wants that to happen! But the scary truth is, it actually can. Gaping holes can simply open up in the ground and swallow whatever is on top. They're called sinkholes, or cenotes.

Sinkholes are a horribly frightening idea. We expect the ground beneath our feet to stay where it is, and be solid and reliable. It's not a pleasant thought that it could suddenly just ... disappear!

WHY SINKHOLES HAPPEN

THERE ARE ACTUALLY SEVERAL DIFFERENT THINGS THAT CAN CREATE A SINKHOLE. SOME ARE NATURAL, AND SOME ARE CAUSED BY HUMAN ACTIVITIES.

THE NATURAL TYPE HAPPEN WHEN THE GROUND IS GRADUALLY DISSOLVED AWAY BY UNDERGROUND WATER. THIS IS ESPECIALLY LIKELY WHERE THE GROUND IS MADE OF ROCK THAT DISSOLVES EASILY, LIKE LIMESTONE, CHALK, OR SALT. OVER LONG PERIODS OF TIME, UNDERGROUND CAVES OPEN UP. EVENTUALLY, THE LAND OVER THE TOP COLLAPSES DOWN INTO THEM.

IN CITIES, WATER PIPES CAN SOMETIMES CRACK AND LEAK UNDER THE GROUND. THIS CREATES A BIG FLOW OF WATER THAT CAN QUICKLY WASH AWAY UNDERGROUND SAND OR MUD, LEAVING A BIG GAP. ROADS, SIDEWALKS, OR BUILDINGS THAT ARE ABOVE THE GAP CAN THEN CAVE IN, ESPECIALLY WHEN THERE'S EXTRA WEIGHT ON THEM (LIKE A PERSON OR A CAR).

LASTLY, SINKHOLES CAN APPEAR WHERE MINES OR TUNNELS HAVE BEEN DUG UNDERGROUND. THE UNDERGROUND SPACE COLLAPSES, AND SO DOES THE GROUND ON TOP.

Scary SINKHOLES

Not all sinkholes appear suddenly, but when they do, they can be terrifying. They range from really small—sometimes no bigger than a large plate—to absolutely massive. Some can swallow up whole buildings.

In China in 2012, a 70-year-old woman fell down a tiny but deep sinkhole that appeared as she walked along a sidewalk. She was rescued, though she had some broken bones.

A family in Florida, U.S.A., woke up to find a huge, 50-foot (15.2-m)-deep sinkhole had appeared in the lawn right behind their house. Sinkholes are quite common in Florida, and sometimes happen under houses, making them collapse.

Sinkholes can appear in roads too, and sometimes cars or trucks fall down into them. One sinkhole created a deep pit in a road in Manchester, England.

In Bowling Green, Kentucky, U.S.A., a huge sinkhole opened up in the floor of a car museum in 2014. Fortunately, no one was hurt when the 60-foot (18.3-m)-long, 45-foot (13.7-m)-wide, 30-foot (9.1-m)-deep hole suddenly appeared, but it did take with it some pretty precious cargo: eight classic Corvettes! Repairs and damages totaled more than five million dollars, but there was good news: After the disaster, attendance at the museum soared! They even sell jars of rocks and sinkhole dirt in the gift shop.

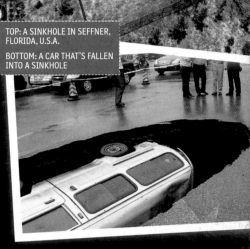

TOP: A SINKHOLE IN SEFFNER, FLORIDA, U.S.A.

BOTTOM: A CAR THAT'S FALLEN INTO A SINKHOLE

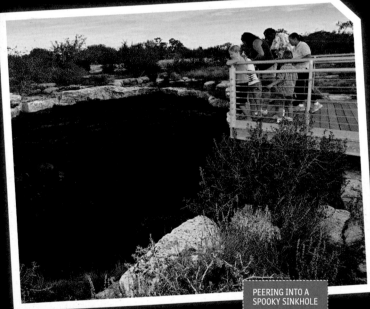

PEERING INTO A SPOOKY SINKHOLE

Ancient SINKHOLES

Those sinkholes appeared recently—but there are also a lot of sinkholes around the world that have been there for hundreds or thousands of years. They include some of the biggest sinkholes of all. The Xiaozhai Tiankeng, or Heavenly Pit, in China, is thought to be one of the deepest, at 2,165 feet (660 m) deep. That's more than half a mile!

The Devil's Sinkhole, in Texas, U.S.A., is an ancient sinkhole about 50 feet (15 m) wide. Below ground, it becomes much wider, opening up into a cavern 320 feet (98 m) wide and 350 feet (107 m) deep. Old sinkholes like this can have their own wildlife—the Devil's Sinkhole is home to huge numbers of bats. They flock out of the hole every evening to go hunting for insects.

Shaky GROUND

So, are you safe from sinkholes? Well, it depends on where you live. Some places, such as Florida, in the United States, are especially prone to sinkholes. They also happen a lot in China, and Guatemala City has had more than its fair share.

The good news is that most sinkholes don't appear in just a few seconds. They often form gradually, and there are usually warning signs. You might see cracks in the ground, or the ground level starting to sink slightly. If the doors or windows of a house become difficult to open and shut, that could mean a sinkhole is growing nearby, making the house tilt slightly.

Overall, the chance of you falling into a sinkhole is pretty small.

SINKHOLE IN GUATEMALA CITY IN 2010

YELLOWSTONE SUPERVOLCANO

UNDER YELLOWSTONE NATIONAL PARK IN WYOMING, U.S.A., LIES A HUMONGOUS ACTIVE VOLCANO. It's so big, it's known as a "supervolcano." If or when it erupts, it could be one of the biggest volcanic eruptions in history, causing disaster across North America and around the world. The last time it really blew its top was 640,000 years ago, and now some scientists say a major eruption is overdue.

FRIGHT-O-METER
DON'T READ THIS BOOK BEFORE BED
UWILLBUPALLN8

FURIOUS FORCES

You might think of a volcano as a tall pointy mountain with smoke coming out of the top. That's often true for smaller volcanoes, such as Mount Arenal in Costa Rica, or Mount Rainier in Washington State, U.S.A. However, some of the biggest volcanoes of all are not mountains—they are calderas.

A caldera is a large, wide, open dish-shaped crater in the ground. The Yellowstone caldera is so big, you can't really even see it when you're standing right on top of it. The supervolcano is not measurable in feet, like most volcanoes—this one is so huge it's measured in miles—roughly 45 miles (72 km) long and 35 miles (56 km) wide. You can also tell the area is volcanic because of its many hot springs, geysers, and fumaroles (jets of steam coming out of the ground). They are caused by the hot magma (molten rock) not far below the surface.

A caldera forms when a massive volcanic eruption blasts out so much lava, rock, dust, and ash, it leaves a big crater behind. That's what happened the last time Yellowstone had a major eruption—and the time before that, and the time before that! These eruptions were thousands or even millions of years ago.

After an eruption, the magma underneath the ground starts to build up, until it's ready to explode again. This explains why, if the Yellowstone supervolcano is sticking to its regular schedule, some scientists think it's ready to go at any moment.

Atmosphere

Yellowstone caldera
Geysers
Earth crust
Earth crust
Magma

YELLOWSTONE
NATIONAL
PARK

NATIONAL
PARK
SERVICE

WHAT WOULD
HAPPEN?

A supervolcano throws out a huge amount of lava and ash when it erupts—more than 240 cubic miles (1,000 cubic km). As a comparison, in 1980, a huge eruption of another volcano, Mount St. Helens, blasted away the whole top of the mountain. The amount of material ejected was only around .67 cubic miles (2.8 cubic km). The last Yellowstone eruption was 350 times bigger than that.

If an eruption like that happened, the ash flung out of the volcano could cover a huge area—some say as much as two-thirds of the United States. This would destroy crops, make houses collapse, clog waterways, bury roads, pollute the air, and, well, basically cause chaos. Large eruptions also send ash and dust into orbit around the planet. This can reduce sunlight for several years, harming plants and animals.

MAJOR VOLCANO ERUPTIONS CAN SPREAD ASH FOR HUNDREDS OF MILES.

TIME TO PANIC!
OR NOT?

STORIES OFTEN APPEAR IN THE MEDIA SAYING THAT YELLOWSTONE IS ABOUT TO BLOW, AND WARNING OF IMPENDING DOOM. BUT THE SCIENTISTS WHO ACTUALLY WORK AT THE YELLOWSTONE VOLCANO OBSERVATORY AREN'T QUITE AS WORRIED. THEY MONITOR THE AREA CAREFULLY, MEASURING AND SCANNING THE GROUND TO SEE IF IT IS BULGING OR SHAKING, WHICH CAN SHOW WHAT THE MAGMA UNDERNEATH IS DOING.

THOUGH THE WHOLE YELLOWSTONE AREA IS VOLCANICALLY ACTIVE, IT DOES NOT APPEAR TO BE CHANGING FAST, OR BUILDING UP TO A BIG ERUPTION AT THE MOMENT. IT COULD HAPPEN SOON, BUT SO FAR, EXPERTS SAY THE CHANCES ARE QUITE SMALL. IT WILL ERUPT AGAIN, BUT THEY SAY IT'S MORE LIKELY TO HAPPEN IN A FEW THOUSAND YEARS THAN RIGHT NOW.

EVEN IF AN ERUPTION WAS COMING, WE WOULD PROBABLY HAVE A FEW WEEKS' OR MONTHS' WARNING, AS THE OBSERVATORY WOULD DETECT THE PRESSURE BUILDING UP UNDERGROUND.

NATIONAL
PARK
SERVICE

VOLCANOES!

THERE ARE SEVERAL VOLCANOES AROUND THE WORLD THAT COULD HAVE A HUGE ERUPTION AND CAUSE HAVOC. BESIDES YELLOWSTONE, THEY INCLUDE MOUNT VESUVIUS IN ITALY, AND POPOCATÉPETL IN MEXICO.

VESUVIUS LOOMS OVER THE CITY OF NAPLES, ITALY.

TECH TAKEOVER

FRIGHT-O-METER
DON'T READ THIS BOOK BEFORE BED
0 1 2 3 4 5 6 7 8 9 10
UWILLBUPAL-N8

YOU'VE PROBABLY SEEN IT BEFORE IN SCI-FI BOOKS AND MOVIES: A FUTURISTIC WORLD IN WHICH INTELLIGENT ROBOTS AND COMPUTERS ARE AS SMART AS HUMANS. Sometimes, they begin to outsmart humans and take over the world themselves. Could that really happen? Some scientists think it could, while others say, "Calm down! Humans could never be replaced by technology!" So ... who's right? The truth is, we don't really know ... yet!

SINGULARITY

Ever since computers were first built, less than 100 years ago, they've been getting smarter, smaller, faster, and more human-like. Some computer scientists specialize in "artificial intelligence"—programming computers to behave in an intelligent way, or to imitate human intelligence. Others work on "artificial life"—building programs or robots that look, act, or behave like real living things. This can be pretty useful—for example, when you want a computer to be able to understand spoken instructions, and speak right back to you.

But it didn't take long before scientists and sci-fi writers realized that maybe, one day, it could all go too far! What if computers got so clever, they could out-think us? What if, instead of just being programmed, they could actually make their own decisions? Even worse, what if they became so advanced, they could make copies of themselves and reproduce, like living things can? Scientists call this moment—when computer intelligence outstrips what we can understand—the "technological singularity." And it doesn't seem like that moment is too far away.

There are now computers that can beat the world's top players at complicated games like chess, and a difficult Chinese board game called "Go." There are computers that can have a lifelike conversation with a real human. There are computers that can rewrite their own programming code, to make themselves work better. Some tech experts think the singularity, and the possibility of machines taking over the world, could be here in just a few years. Others think it might not be so soon, but could happen sometime in the 21st century.

AlphaGo   Lee Sedol

GRAY GOO

YOU MIGHT HAVE HEARD OF "GRAY GOO," A NIGHTMARE SCENARIO IN WHICH NANOBOTS—MICROSCOPICALLY SMALL ROBOTS—OVERRUN THE WORLD. NANOTECHNOLOGY IS DEVELOPING FAST, AND EXPERTS ARE BUILDING VERY SMALL BOTS THAT CAN COLLECT ENERGY FROM THEIR SUR-ROUNDINGS. THE FEAR IS THAT THEY COULD BECOME SELF-REPLICATING— ABLE TO USE THE MATERIALS AROUND THEM TO MAKE MORE AND MORE NANOBOTS. THIS COULD RUN OUT OF CONTROL, SO THAT EVERYTHING ON EARTH WOULD END UP "EATEN" AND TRANSFORMED INTO A SLUDGE OF GAZILLIONS OF NANOBOTS.

BUT MANY SCIENTISTS HAVE POINTED OUT IT WOULD BE REALLY HARD FOR THE BOTS TO EXTRACT THE RIGHT INGREDIENTS TO DO THIS FROM EXISTING OBJECTS. IN ANY GIVEN AREA, THEY WOULD PROBABLY RUN OUT OF THE RIGHT "FOOD" PRETTY QUICKLY. AFTER ALL, WE ALREADY HAVE MANY SPECIES OF BACTERIA THAT WORK IN EXACTLY THIS WAY. AND THEY HAVEN'T TAKEN OVER THE WORLD AND TURNED IT ALL INTO BACTERIA (YET).

SOME SCIENTISTS HAVE SAID GRAY GOO COULD EVEN TAKE OVER OTHER PLANETS—FOR EXAMPLE, IF THE NANOBOTS ESCAPED INTO SPACE ON A ROCKET OR SPACE PROBE.

OVERLORDS

Of course, a laptop sitting on your desk cannot get up and take over the world— however smart its software is. It can't move or actually do anything to you. However, that's not all there is to computers. There are also computer-controlled robots, and computer networks, which link computers together. Increasingly, there's also the "Internet of things," which connects things like buildings, cars, power stations, or hospital equipment to the Internet.

If computer software did become conscious and decided to attack humans, it's possible that it could work through systems like these to take control. Computers and robots might eventually be able to make more computers and robots, until they overpowered humanity.

Manpower

It sounds pretty scary! But before you start losing sleep over it, remember that some scientists think there's nothing to worry about. Humans invented computers, and we program them. At the moment, they run on electricity, which we con-trol as well. If anything like this did ever start to happen, we could probably shut the systems down before the situation got out of hand At least, we hope so!

135

MARTIAN MANIA

MARS IS ONE OF THE CLOSET PLANETS TO EARTH, AND ONE OF THE MOST SIMILAR. People have often thought the most likely aliens would be "Martians"—often imagined as small, green, human-shaped creatures. So, since humans first started began to search the sky with telescopes, we've been looking for life on Mars. Quite a few times, it seemed like we'd found it! But have we?

DON'T READ THIS BOOK BEFORE BED

0 1 2 3 4 5 6 7 8 9 10

FRIGHT-O-METER

UWILL 3UPALLN8

GIOVANNI SCHIAPARELLI

MARTIAN
CANALS

IN THE 1870S, ITALIAN ASTRONOMER GIOVANNI SCHIAPARELLI THOUGHT HE SAW LONG LINES OR CHANNELS ON THE SURFACE OF MARS, THROUGH HIS TELESCOPE. He named them canali, Italian for "channels." But another astronomer, Percival Lowell, thought they really were canals—artificial waterways that someone had built.

Lowell studied the "canals" of Mars for years. He decided that intelligent, civilized Martians must have built the canals to deliver water around their planet as it began to dry out.

Other space scientists, though, claimed they couldn't see any canals. Eventually, as telescopes improved, it turned out that the lines weren't really there. They were an optical illusion created by looking at the random features of Mars through early, low-power telescopes.

FACE

IN 1976, THE NASA SPACE PROBE VIKING 1 WAS ORBITING MARS AND TOOK SEVERAL PICTURES OF ITS SURFACE. Astronomers noticed that one of these showed a huge human-looking face carved into the surface! Or did it?

The "Face on Mars" was a sensation around the world when it was shown on TV and in newspapers. It REALLY looks like a human face, a mask, or maybe a sci-fi-style space helmet. Lots of people were sure it was some kind of monument built by the Martians. They also thought it showed that Martians must have a human-like appearance, or had been visited by humans in the past.

However, scientists argued that it probably wasn't a deliberate face picture, just a natural rock formation with sharp shadows that made it look like a face. In 1998, another probe, Mars Global Surveyor, was able to fly over the "face" again and take clearer images. It didn't look quite so face-like this time.

ABOVE: ERODED ROCKS ON MARS RESEMBLE A HUMAN FACE.

RIGHT: IMAGE OF MARS'S SURFACE TAKEN BY NASA'S RECONAISSANCE ORBITER

TREES

IN 2010, ASTRONOMERS RELEASED ANOTHER IMAGE CAPTURED BY A PROBE ORBITING MARS. This time, it seemed to show dark green trees sprouting from the surface! In fact, though, it's an optical illusion. The "trees" are actually trails of darker sand that have rolled down sand dunes. This happens in the Martian springtime, as frozen carbon dioxide gas evaporates.

PAREIDOLIA

PARE-WHAT? THIS WEIRD WORD IS PRONOUNCED "PAIR-I-DOH-LEE-A," AND IT MEANS OUR NATURAL ABILITY TO SEE FAMILIAR SHAPES IN RANDOM PATTERNS—ESPECIALLY FACES. THE HUMAN BRAIN NATURALLY COMPARES WHAT IT SEES TO ITS MEMORIES, AND TRIES TO MAKE MATCHES. THAT'S ESPECIALLY TRUE FOR FACES AND HUMAN FIGURES, AS WE ARE ALWAYS INTERACTING WITH EACH OTHER.

SO IF YOU SHOW SOMEONE A RANDOM PATTERN OF MARKINGS, SHADOWS, OR SHAPES, THEY'LL PROBABLY PICK OUT SOMETHING THAT LOOKS LIKE A FACE, A HAND, OR A WHOLE HUMAN. "FACES" OR OTHER FAMILIAR SHAPES SPOTTED ON MARS ARE THE RESULT OF JUST A FEW OF MILLIONS OF IMAGES HAPPENING TO RESEMBLE SOMETHING WE RECOGNIZE.

THIS HOUSE HAS A FACE!

THE MARTIAN METEORITE

IN 1986, EXPLORERS IN ANTARCTICA FOUND A METEORITE—A ROCK THAT HAS FALLEN FROM SPACE. From the chemicals it contained, they figured out that it probably came from Mars, and was blasted into space by an asteroid impact millions of years ago. Inside the rock, scans revealed microscopic wormlike shapes. Some scientists think they could be fossils of ancient bacteria-like living things.

We're still studying Mars, and experts are pretty sure it did, and probably still does, have liquid water on it. That means life could exist there. If it does, though, it probably isn't the little green men you'd hoped for. It's more likely to be tiny creatures, similar to our bacteria or algae.

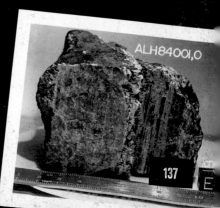

ALH84001,0

FLOATING FREE

SOMETHING VERY WEIRD IS HAPPEN-ING. You're floating up into the air, so high that your nose is almost touching the ceiling. Then you look down—and you can see someone lying there, far below you. Who is it? Wait a minute— it's YOU! But if that's you down there—what are you doing up here!?

This bizarre sensation is known as an out-of-body experience, or OBE. Although it's strange, it actually happens to quite a lot of people. Around 10 percent of the population will have an OBE at some time in their lives, and a few people have them repeatedly.

DON'T READ THIS BOOK BEFORE BED

0 1 2 3 4 5 6 7 8 9 10

FRIGHT-O-METER

UWILLBUPALLN8

SOME PEOPLE BELIEVE IN "ASTRAL PROJECTION"— A FORM OF OUT-OF-BODY EXPERIENCE DURING WHICH YOU CAN TRAVEL LONG DISTANCES, EVEN TO OTHER PLANETS.

OUT-OF-BODY ODDITY

Most people who have an OBE describe very similar things. They have a strong sense of floating out of their own body, often upward into the air. Their mind, or their "point of view," seems to move away from their physical body, and they can often see the room or the place they are in from a completely new angle. And sometimes, they also get a view of the body they have left behind—their own body.

OBEs can happen in a variety of situations, usually when a person is asleep or unconscious for some reason. It could be:

- ➲ When someone faints
- ➲ When they're halfway between being awake and falling asleep
- ➲ When they're unconscious on an operating table
- ➲ When they're short of oxygen, such as a person who is suffering altitude sickness on a high mountain
- ➲ Or when an accident knocks them unconscious

NEAR-DEATH EXPERIENCES

Some of the weirdest OBEs happen when someone almost dies—like when they have a heart attack and their heart stops beating for a while. They often describe floating upward, or along a tunnel, seeing a bright light, and feeling a sense of love and calmness. Sometimes they sense that someone is telling them they have to go back—then they drop back into their body again and wake up.

DREAM OR REALITY?

The big question is, does the person really go "out" of their body? Can the soul, spirit, or mind actually separate from your body and go somewhere else? Or is it just something you imagine—an illusion caused by your brain?

One way to tell would be if people could see things while "floating around" in an OBE, which they could not have known about otherwise. And that brings us to ...

MARIA'S SHOE

One of the most famous OBEs of all dates from 1977, when a patient named Maria suffered a heart attack. While in the hospital her heart stopped, but she recovered and woke up. She told a social worker she had an out-of-body experience, during which she floated up to the ceiling, then outside through the wall. On a ledge of the building, she saw an old, worn tennis shoe, which she described in detail. She begged the social worker to find out if it was really there. It was!

However, investigators later put a shoe in the same place, and found it could be seen from some of the hospital's windows. They claimed Maria must have seen it, or heard people talking about it, then dreamed about it during her OBE.

A convincing case, or a sensible explanation?

TESTING, TESTING!

THE STRANGE CASE OF MARIA'S SHOE IS HARD TO PROVE, BUT SCIENTISTS AND HOSPITALS HAVE SET UP THEIR OWN EXPERIMENTS TO SEE IF OBES ARE REAL. USUALLY THEY PUT WORDS OR SYMBOLS FACING UPWARD ON HIGH SHELVES, OR ON PIECES OF CARD SUSPENDED FROM THE CEILING. SO FAR, NO ONE HAS CONVINCINGLY REPORTED SEEING THEM.

IN ONE CASE, A SCIENTIST STUDIED A WOMAN WHO OFTEN HAD OBEs IN HER SLEEP. HE HID A SECRET FIVE-FIGURE NUMBER ABOVE HER BED AND SHE LATER REPORTED THE NUMBER CORRECTLY. HOWEVER, THE SCIENTIST ADMITTED SHE FELL ASLEEP DURING THE TEST, SO SHE COULD HAVE PEEKED.

THE END OF THE WORLD

IT'S THE DAY DOOMSDAY PREPPERS EVERYWHERE ARE WAITING FOR. The day something wipes out the world's population, leaving behind only those who have hunkered down in bunkers below Earth's surface. People have been convinced the world is ending since history began, and they've always been wrong. Well, so far, anyway. But could the world, or life on Earth, come to an end one day? It certainly could. In fact, it certainly WILL. The question is how ... and when? Run for cover as we walk you through the top scenarios for the end of life as we know it.

DON'T READ THIS BOOK BEFORE BED
0 1 2 3 4 5 6 7 8 9 10
FRIGHT-O-METER
UWILLBUPALL. 8

OH NO! ASTEROID ALERT!

ROCK-AND-Roll

Asteroids are lumps of rock that orbit around the sun, like mini-planets. There are millions of them zooming around our solar system, ranging from the size of a bus to more than 600 miles (966 km) across. Most of them are far away. But sometimes an asteroid comes close enough to Earth to be a danger. If a really big one smashed into our planet, it could cause all kinds of horrendous disasters ...

➲ Massive destruction wherever the asteroid landed

➲ Giant tsunamis that could swamp major cities

➲ Years of darkness and cold, thanks to debris flying into orbit and blocking out sunlight

➲ Terrible droughts, as the lack of heat from the sun would also mean less water evaporating to form clouds, and much less rain

➲ These things would lead to major crop failures and famines.

Going EXTINCT

A large asteroid, around 6 to 10 miles (10 to 16 km) across, could wipe out most of Earth's living things. In fact, that's probably what happened 65 million years ago, when a big asteroid is thought to have hit Yucatán, Mexico. This is the leading theory for the disappearance of dinosaurs, and many other prehistoric animals.

Scarfed by THE SUN

Whatever happens, we know for sure that Earth will not be around forever. We depend on our star, the sun, to give us the heat and light we need to survive. But as the sun becomes an old star, it will grow bigger and hotter, turning into what space scientists call a red giant. Eventually, it will get SO big, it will swallow up its nearest planets, Mercury, Venus, and Earth. Long before that, though, its sizzling heat will dry up Earth's oceans and destroy all life.

DANGER FACTOR? Don't panic! Fortunately, this isn't scheduled to happen for roughly another seven billion years. By then, if we're still around, humans will have probably figured out a way to go and live on another friendly planet somewhere else.

SORRY, EARTH ... TIME'S UP!

RADIOACTIVE
Rays

Gamma rays are a type of powerful radiation energy. They are released by nuclear explosions, and are very harmful to life. They also come from outer space, when collapsing stars create enormous explosions that blast gamma rays across the universe. Scientists often detect these "gamma ray bursts" in other galaxies, but they are mostly much too far away to harm us.

However, if one happened in our galaxy, the Milky Way, and was pointing right at us, it could seriously mess up Earth's atmosphere, and poison our planet with nuclear radiation. This could wipe out some, or all, of life on Earth.

DANGER FACTOR? You can relax! Scientists have calculated that the chances of a gamma ray burst happening in our galaxy are only around 0.1 percent, or 1 in 1,000. The chance that it could also be pointing right at us is so unlikely, it will probably never happen. Phew!

ASTEROID SPOTTING

TO TRY TO DEAL WITH THE RISK OF AN ASTEROID STRIKE, WE USE OUR POWERFUL TELESCOPES TO LOOK OUT FOR ANY ASTEROIDS THAT MIGHT FLY CLOSE TO EARTH. SO FAR, SCIENTISTS HAVE FOUND MORE THAN 800 OF THEM. THEY WATCH THEM CAREFULLY AND CALCULATE THE PATH THEY WILL FOLLOW. AT THE MOMENT, THEY THINK THERE'S ONLY A TINY RISK—LESS THAN A 1 IN 1,000 CHANCE—OF A DANGEROUS ASTEROID HITTING US IN THE NEXT 100 YEARS.

IF IT LOOKED AS IF A BIG ASTEROID WAS ON A COLLISION COURSE, WE MIGHT EVEN BE ABLE TO STOP IT. WE COULD SEND A SPACECRAFT TO MEET IT AND SET OFF AN EXPLOSION THAT WOULD PUSH IT OFF COURSE, SO THAT IT WOULD MISS EARTH.

DANGER FACTOR? AS FAR AS WE KNOW, NO LARGE ASTEROIDS ARE ON A COLLISION COURSE WITH US RIGHT NOW. BUT THEN IT ISN'T ALWAYS EASY TO SEE THEM COMING. FINGERS CROSSED!

A GAMMA RAY ... BUT IT'S NOT POINTING OUR WAY!

EXPERTS THINK A MASSIVE ASTEROID IMPACT WITH EARTH PROBABLY CREATED OUR MOON MORE THAN FOUR BILLION YEARS AGO. IT FORMED FROM ALL THE ROCK THROWN INTO ORBIT AFTER THE COLLISION.

PHOTO CREDITS

FRONT COVER: (UP LE), CPM PHOTO/Shutterstock; (CTR LE), iStock.com/Frank Boellmann; (LO LE), Hemis/Alamy Stock Photo; (LO CTR), Konstantin Kalishko/Alamy Stock Photo; (LO RT), Prezoom.nl/Shutterstock. **SPINE:** adike/Shutterstock. **BACK COVER:** (CTR LE), Barry Mansell/NPL/Minden Pictures; (LO LE), MichaelTaylor3d/Shutterstock

INTERIOR: 3 (CTR RT), Barry Mansell/NPL/Minden Pictures; 4 (LE), Shaul Schwarz/Getty Images; 4 (RT), Gary Doan/Alamy Stock Photo; 5 (UP), Belizar/Shutterstock; 5 (LE), Vukkostic/Getty Images; 5 (RT), photoDISC; 6 (LE), adike/Shutterstock; 6 (UP RT), Isselee/Dreamstime; 6 (LO RT), Prezoom.nl/Shutterstock; 7 (LE), Alex Roz/Shutterstock; 7 (UP RT), Stocksnapper/Shutterstock; 8-9 (BACKGROUND), RGB Ventures/SuperStock/Alamy Stock Photo; 8 (CTR RT), Profimedia.CZ a.s./Alamy Stock Photo; 9 (UP), isifa Image Service s.r.o./Alamy Stock Photo; 9 (CTR RT), imageBROKER/Alamy Stock Photo; 9 (LO CTR), lynea/Shutterstock; 9 (LO RT), vukkostic/Getty Images; 10-11 (BACKGROUND), Konstantin Kalishko/Alamy Stock Photo; 10 (LO), Wyatt Rivard/Shutterstock; 11 (UP), Hemis/Alamy Stock Photo; 11 (CTR RT), Africa Studio/Shutterstock; 11 (LO LE), EmmePi Images/Alamy Stock Photo; 12-13 (BACKGROUND), Elegeyda/Shutterstock; 13 (LE), Ashley Watts Photography; 13 (CTR RT), Mothman Museum, WV; 13 (LO), Eric Isselee/Shutterstock; 14-15 (BACKGROUND), Danita Delimont/Alamy Stock Photo; 14 (LO RT), Key West Art & Historical Society; 14 (LO CTR), Key West Art & Historical Society; 15 (LE), Key West Art & Historical Society; 15 (RT), robertharding/Alamy Stock Photo; 16-17 (BACKGROUND), Raymond Wong/National Geographic Creative; 16 (LO), Emory Kristof/National Geographic Creative; 17 (UP RT), Universal History Archive/Getty Images; 18-19 (BACKGROUND), Karuka/Shutterstock; 18 (LO), Ana Thomas/Shutterstock; 19 (UP), g215/Shutterstock; 19 (CTR), Keith Szafranski/Getty Images; 19 (LO), EFKS/Shutterstock; 20-21 (BACKGROUND), Neil Overy/Arcangel Images; 20 (CTR RT), SOBEPS/COBEPS; 20 (LO), UK Ministry of Defence; 21 (CTR RT), Glazyuk/Dreamstime; 21 (LO), Top Vector Studio/Shutterstock; 22 (LO LE), isifa Image Service s.r.o./Alamy Stock Photo; 22 (LO CTR), The Marsden Archive/Alamy Stock Photo; 22 (LO RT), Stock Connection Blue/Alamy Stock Photo; 23 (UP RT), a003771/Shutterstock; 23 (CTR RT), Jonathan Blair/National Geographic Creative; 23 (LO RT), Orhan Cam/Shutterstock; 23 (LO LE), Hemis/Alamy Stock Photo; 24-25 (BACKGROUND), Don Mammoser/Shutterstock; 24 (LO), Bates Littlehales/National Geographic Creative; 25 (UP LE), George Steinmetz/National Geographic Creative; 25 (UP CTR), adike/Shutterstock; 25 (LO LE), Angelinast/Shutterstock; 25 (LO RT), Shaul Schwarz/Getty Images; 26-27 (BACKGROUND), Murdo MacLeod/Polaris; 26 (LO CTR), Murdo MacLeod/Polaris; 26 (LO LE), NG Maps; 27 (UP RT), Courtesy Steven Gibbons; 27 (LO RT), Hadel Productions/Getty Images; 28-29 (BACKGROUND), Nednae/Dreamstime; 28 (LE), Verity Johnson/Shutterstock; 28 (RT), Colicaranica/Dreamstime; 29 (RT), United States Patent Office; 30 (RT), Gareth Dewar/Alamy Stock Photo; 31 (UP), Keystone/Getty Images; 31 (CTR), Courtesy of ECHO, Leahy Center for Lake Champlain; 31 (LO LE), Canada Post Corporation; 31 (LO RT), Michael Taylor 3D/Shutterstock; 32-33 (BACKGROUND), Steve Baxter; 32 (LO), Mary Evans Picture Library/Alamy Stock Photo; 33 (UP), Gmnicholas/Getty Images; 33 (LO), John North/Getty Images; 34-35 (BACKGROUND), Melanie Hoffman/Dreamstime; 35 (UP LE), Michele Cornelius/Dreamstime; 35 (UP RT), Eric Isselee/Dreamstime; 35 (LO LE), Jason Horne; 35 (LO CTR), Meoita/Shutterstock; 35 (LO RT), Bruno Guenard/Minden Pictures; 36 (LO), PhotoQuest/Getty Images; 37 (UP LE), Jim West/Alamy Stock Photo; 37 (UP RT), Sergey Panychev/Shutterstock; 37 (CTR), Ian Grant/Alamy Stock Photo; 38-39 (BACKGROUND), Hemis/Alamy Stock Photo; 38 (UP RT), CraigRJD/Getty Images; 38 (LO), Universal Pictures/Legendary/REX/Shutterstock; 39 (UP RT), Ionut David/Alamy Stock Photo; 39 (CTR), Universal History Archive/Getty Images; 40-41 (BACKGROUND), Tony Watson/Alamy Stock Photo; 40 (LO), Matthijs Wetterauw/Alamy Stock Photo; 41 (UP LE), Sabena Jane Blackbird/Alamy Stock Photo; 41 (CTR RT), Chris Mattison/Minden Pictures; 41 (LO LE), BrAt82/Shutterstock; 42-43 (BACKGROUND), Anton Ivanov/Shutterstock; 42 (LO LE), Universal History Archive/Getty Images; 42 (LO RT), Kenneth Garrett/National Geographic Creative; 43 (UP LE), Kenneth Garrett/National Geographic Creative; 43 (UP RT), Gary Warnimont/Alamy Stock Photo; 43 (LO RT), Pictorial Press Ltd/Alamy Stock Photo; 43 (LO LE), Art Directors & TRIP/Alamy Stock Photo; 44-45 (BACKGROUND), Maxiphoto/Getty Images; 44 (LO RT), Eric Isselee/Shutterstock; 45 (UP LE), Mark William Penny/Shutterstock; 45 (UP RT), Katie Smit Photography/Shutterstock; 45 (CTR RT), Boule/Shutterstock; 45 (LO RT), AP Photo; 46-47 (BACKGROUND), IgorZh/Getty Images; 46 (LO), bonottomario/Getty Images; 47 (UP LE), Pixeljoy/Shutterstock; 47 (CTR RT), Jim Henderson/Alamy Stock Photo; 47 (CTR LE), Rob Atkins/Getty Images; 47 (LO), Loeser Collection/Art Resource, NY; 48-49 (BACKGROUND), abadonian/Getty Images; 48 (LO), Courtesy J.W. Ocker; 49 (UP LE), Chris Hellier/Alamy Stock Photo; 49 (UP RT), Stockphoto Mania/Shutterstock; 49 (UP CTR RT), Lena_graphics/Shutterstock; 48 (LO CTR RT), Barcroft/Getty Images; 49 (LO RT), Stephen Frink; 50 (UP), Strixcode/Dreamstime; 50 (LO LE), Donald Gargano/Shutterstock; 50 (LO RT), belizar/Shutterstock; 51 (UP CTR), rudall30/Shutterstock; 51 (UP RT), Shafran/Shutterstock; 51 (CTR RT), rudall30/Shutterstock; 51 (CTR LE), Debbie Jew Clark/Shutterstock; 52-53 (BACKGROUND), Satori13/Dreamstime; 52 (CTR RT), Lonely/Shutterstock; 53 (LE), Mary Evans Picture Library/Alamy Stock Photo; 53 (RT), Coneyl Jay/Science Photo Library; 54-55 (BACKGROUND), Godrick/Dreamstime.com; 54 (LO LE), Lindsay Smith/Alamy Stock Photo; 54 (LO RT), Lespalenik/Dreamstime.com; 55 (UP), Gary Doak/Alamy Stock Photo; 55 (LO), Gary Doan/Alamy Stock Photo; 56-57 (BACKGROUND), Kichigin/Shutterstock; 56 (LO), Alfio Scisetti/Alamy Stock Photo; 57 (UP), boydz1980/Getty Images; 57 (UP INSET), Shunfa Teh/Shutterstock; 57 (CTR), Anton Brand/Shutterstock; 57 (LO), epa european pressphoto agency b.v./Alamy Stock Photo; 58-59 (BACKGROUND), Myper/Shutterstock; 58 (CTR), 2203549/Getty Images; 58 (LO), GL Archive/Alamy Stock Photo; 59 (UP), Nigel Hicks/National Geographic Creative; 59 (CTR), Cogent/Dreamstime; 59 (LO), John Erickson/Shutterstock; 60-61 (BACKGROUND), Noradoa/Shutterstock; 60 (LO), Albertoloyo/Dreamstime; 61 (UP), Cathy Keifer/Shutterstock; 61 (LO), David Carillet/Shutterstock; 62-63 (BACKGROUND), SMC Images/Getty Images; 62 (CTR LE), Zinni-Online/Getty Images; 62 (CTR RT), Jurgen Freund/Minden Pictures; 63 (UP LE), Fritz Polking/Minden Pictures; 63 (UP RT), Vector Tradition/Shutterstock; 63 (CTR RT), Jannarong/Shutterstock; 63 (LO RT), arka38/Shutterstock; 64-65 (BACKGROUND), Sellingpix/Dreamstime; 64 (LO LE), Steve Vidler/Alamy Stock Photo; 65 (LO RT), Pictures from History/Woodbury & Page/Bridgeman Images; 66 (LE), CHAIWATPHOTOS/Shutterstock; 66 (RT), Sebastian Kaulitzki/Shutterstock; 67 (UP RT), Helder Almeida/Dreamstime; 67 (CTR RT), Eivaisla/Shutterstock; 67 (LO RT), DeymosHR/Shutterstock; 67 (LO LE), Aetmeister/Dreamstime; 67 (CTR LE), rangizzz/Shutterstock; 68-69 (BACKGROUND), Jules Gervais Courtellemont/National Geographic Creative; 69 (UP), Sergiejew/Shutterstock; 69 (LO), Trinity Mirror/Mirrorpix/Alamy Stock Photo; 70-71 (BACKGROUND), Babak Tafreshi/Science Source; 70 (LO RT), Mehau Kulyk/Science Source; 71 (UP), Hurst Photo/Shutterstock; 71 (CTR), Olga Miltsova/Shutterstock; 71 (LO), Detlev Van Ravenswaay/Science Photo Library; 72-73 (BACKGROUND), Nikolay_Popov/Getty Images; 72 (LO), Jim Clare/Minden Pictures; 73 (UP LE), Barry Mansell/Minden Pictures; 73 (UP RT), Michael and Patricia Fogden/Minden Pictures; 73 (LO RT), Patrick Swan/Dreamstime; 74-75 (BACKGROUND), aslysun/Shutterstock; 74 (CTR), Morphart Creation/Shutterstock; 74 (LO), Rosa Jay/Shutterstock; 75 (UP CTR), Granger.com—All rights reserved; 75 (UP RT), French School/Getty Images; 75 (CTR LE),

For Albie and Io—A.C.

The publisher gratefully acknowledges everyone who worked to make this book come together: Anna Claybourne, writer; Becky Baines, project editor; Sarah Mock, photo editor; Amanda Larsen, design director; Kerri Sarembock, designer; Michaela Weglinski, editorial assistant; Gus Tello, design production assistant; Anne LeongSon, design production assistant; Sally Abbey, managing editor; Alix Inchausti, production editor; Larry Shea, copy editor; and Lorna Notsch, proofreader.

Since 1888, the National Geographic Society has funded more than 12,000 research, exploration, and preservation projects around the world. The Society receives funds from National Geographic Partners, LLC, funded in part by your purchase. A portion of the proceeds from this book supports this vital work. To learn more, visit natgeo.com/info.

NATIONAL GEOGRAPHIC and Yellow Border Design are trademarks of the National Geographic Society, used under license.

For more information, visit nationalgeographic.com, call 1-800-647-5463, or write to the following address:

National Geographic Partners
1145 17th Street N.W.
Washington, D.C. 20036-4688 U.S.A.

Visit us online at nationalgeographic.com/books

For librarians and teachers: ngchildrensbooks.org

More for kids from National Geographic: kids.nationalgeographic.com

For information about special discounts for bulk purchases, please contact National Geographic Books Special Sales: specialsales@natgeo.com

For rights or permissions inquiries, please contact National Geographic Books Subsidiary Rights: bookrights@natgeo.com

Art directed by Amanda Larsen
Design Style by Rachel Hamm Plett
Designed by Kerri Sarembock

Trade paperback ISBN: 978-1-4263-2841-1
Reinforced library binding ISBN: 978-1-4263-2842-8

Printed in China
17/RRDS/1